I0438642

FINAL

U.S. Department
of Transportation

**Research and
Special Programs
Administration**

Acadia National Park: Assessment of Alternate Transportation for Schoodic Peninsula

Prepared for:

U.S. Department of the Interior
National Park Service
Acadia National Park

Bar Harbor, Maine

Prepared by:

U.S. Department of Transportation
Research and Special Programs Administration
John A. Volpe National Transportation Systems Center

Cambridge, Massachusetts

November 2002

REPORT DOCUMENTATION PAGE

Form Approved
OMB No. 0704-0188

The public reporting burden for this collection of information is estimated to average 1 hour per response, including the time for reviewing instructions, searching existing data sources, gathering and maintaining the data needed, and completing and reviewing the collection of information. Send comments regarding this burden estimate or any other aspect of this collection of information, including suggestions for reducing the burden, to Department of Defense, Washington Headquarters Services, Directorate for Information Operations and Reports (0704-0188), 1215 Jefferson Davis Highway, Suite 1204, Arlington, VA 22202-4302. Respondents should be aware that notwithstanding any other provision of law, no person shall be subject to any penalty for failing to comply with a collection of information if it does not display a currently valid OMB control number.
PLEASE DO NOT RETURN YOUR FORM TO THE ABOVE ADDRESS.

1. REPORT DATE *(DD-MM-YYYY)*	2. REPORT TYPE	3. DATES COVERED *(From - To)*
11/2001	Planning Study	NA

4. TITLE AND SUBTITLE	5a. CONTRACT NUMBER
Acadia National Park: Assessment of Alternate Transportation for Schoodic Peninsula	NA
	5b. GRANT NUMBER
	NA
	5c. PROGRAM ELEMENT NUMBER
	NA

6. AUTHOR(S)	5d. PROJECT NUMBER
Dyer, Michael G; Peterson, Scott A; Crikelair, Tom	PMIS 89897
	5e. TASK NUMBER
	NPS TIC No. D-303
	5f. WORK UNIT NUMBER
	NA

7. PERFORMING ORGANIZATION NAME(S) AND ADDRESS(ES)	8. PERFORMING ORGANIZATION REPORT NUMBER
U.S. Department of Transportation Research and Special Programs Administration John A. Volpe National Transportation Systems Center	NA

9. SPONSORING/MONITORING AGENCY NAME(S) AND ADDRESS(ES)	10. SPONSOR/MONITOR'S ACRONYM(S)
National Park Service Alternative Transportation Program 1201 Eye St. NW Washington, DC 20005	WASO/ATP
	11. SPONSOR/MONITOR'S REPORT NUMBER(S)
	(see 5d. and 5e. above)

12. DISTRIBUTION/AVAILABILITY STATEMENT

Public distribution/availability.

13. SUPPLEMENTARY NOTES

This report addresses alternative transportation decision factors as indicated below (Y/N/NA):
(N) Non-construction options; (Y) park carrying capacity; (Y) life-cycle/ops. & maintenance costs; (N) cost-effectiveness.

14. ABSTRACT

The National Park Service is developing reuse alternatives in anticipation of the U.S. Navy's turnover of its base on Big Moose Island on Schoodic Peninsula. This report identifies and assesses alternate transportation alternatives to help ensure that the Park meets its goal of maintaining the quiet and scenic condition of the Schoodic parkland. The transportation alternatives considered include combinations of ferry services from Bar Harbor to Winter Harbor, properly linked bus services at each terminal as well as for a substitute for ferry service, enhancements of bicycling opportunities, and provision of park and ride facilities. The report also includes an assessment of roadway impacts in and around the Schoodic parkland resulting from the reuse and implementation of the transportation alternatives.

15. SUBJECT TERMS

Acadia National Park, Schoodic Peninsula, alternate transportation, ferry, bicycle, bus, reuse

16. SECURITY CLASSIFICATION OF:			17. LIMITATION OF ABSTRACT	18. NUMBER OF PAGES	19a. NAME OF RESPONSIBLE PERSON
a. REPORT	b. ABSTRACT	c. THIS PAGE	NA	89	Gary T. Ritter
None	None	None			**19b. TELEPHONE NUMBER** *(Include area code)* 617-494-2716, ritter@volpe.dot.gov

Reset

Standard Form 298 (Rev. 8/98)
Prescribed by ANSI Std. Z39.18

Acadia National Park: Assessment of Alternate Transportation for Schoodic Peninsula

Michael G. Dyer
Scott A. Peterson
Tom Crikelair

November 2001

Prepared by

U.S. Department of Transportation
Research and Special Programs Administration
John A. Volpe National Transportation Systems Center

Prepared for

U.S. Department of the Interior
National Park Service
Acadia National Park

Acknowledgements

The authors wish to thank the numerous organizations and individuals who graciously provided their time, knowledge and guidance in the development of this report. Those of particular note are listed below.

Stakeholders

Paul Haertel, Superintendent (National Park Service, Acadia National Park)
Len Bobinchock, Deputy Superintendent (National Park Service, Acadia National Park)
John Kelly (National Park Service , Acadia National Park)
Bob Holzheimer (National Park Service)

Ronald L. Roy (Maine State Department of Transportation, Office of Passenger Transportation)
James H. Fisher (Hancock County Planning Commission)
Jean Marshall (Eastern Maine Development Corporation)
Roger Barto (Town of Winter Harbor)
Linda Pagels (Town of Gouldsboro)

Mark Brent (Bar Harbor Whale Watcher)
Steven Pagels (Bar Harbor Ferries)
Robert Bowman (Center for Coastal Studies)

Staff and Others

Robert Hallett (U.S. Department of Transportation, Volpe Center)
Luis Sirotsky (U.S. Department of Transportation, Volpe Center)

Table of Contents

1   **Introduction**   1

1.1 **Purpose of Report**   1

1.2 **National Park Service Objectives**   1

1.3 **Navy Base Closure**   1

  1.3.1 *Schoodic Point Base*   1

  1.3.2 *Winter Harbor Housing*   2

1.4 **Park Service Alternate Transportation Program**   2

1.5 **Candidate Transportation Services**   2

1.6 **Organization of Report**   3

2   **Background**   5

2.1 **Description of Area**   5

  2.1.1 *Acadia National Park*   5

  2.1.2 *Schoodic Peninsula*   5

    2.1.2.1   Parkland   5

    2.1.2.2   Gouldsboro and Winter Harbor   6

    2.1.2.3   Navy base   6

    2.1.2.4   Area roads   7

2.2 **Reuse Alternatives**   7

  2.2.1 *Reuse Concept 1*   7

  2.2.2 *Reuse Concept 2*   7

  2.2.3 *Reuse Concept 3*   8

3   **Approach**   9

3.1 **General**   9

3.2 **Transportation Alternatives**   9

  3.2.1 *Ferry services*   10

    3.2.1.1   Commuter and recreational markets   10

    3.2.1.2   Vessel selection   11

    3.2.1.3   Terminals   11

    3.2.1.4   Ferry Service Cost and Revenue Model   11

3.3 Travel Demand Analysis		12
3.3.1 Overview of data resources		12
3.3.1.1	Population	12
3.3.1.2	Employment and journey to work data	13
3.3.1.3	National Park visitation and survey data	14
3.3.1.4	Base reuse analysis	15
3.3.2 Demand modeling process		15
3.3.2.1	Trip generation	15
3.3.2.2	Trip distribution	16
3.3.2.3	Model split	16
3.3.2.4	Assignment	16
3.4 Demand for Ferry Service		17
3.4.1 Data resources		17
3.4.2 Modeling process		17
3.5 Bicycleway Enhancements & Usage		18
3.5.1 Data resources and analysis		18
3.5.2 Park-and-ride assessment		18
3.6 Analysis of Roadway Traffic		19
3.6.1 Data resources		19
3.6.2 Analysis		19
3.7 Bus Services		19
4 Demographics, Land Use, and Park Visitation		21
4.1 Demographics		21
4.1.1 Population		21
4.1.2 Employment		21
4.2 Land Use		23
4.2.1 Winter Harbor		23
4.2.2 Gouldsboro		24
4.3 Park Use		24
5 Ferry Service		27
5.1 Overview		27
5.1.1 Current conditions		27

	5.1.2 *Integration with other projects and studies*	27
5.2	**Candidate Terminals**	29
	5.2.1 *Schoodic Peninsula*	29
	5.2.1.1 South Gouldsboro dock (private)	29
	5.2.1.2 Winter Harbor	30
	5.2.1.3 Sorrento Town dock	32
	5.2.1.4 Summary	32
	5.2.2 *Bar Harbor*	33
5.3	**Candidate Routes**	35
	5.3.1 *Bar Harbor to South Gouldsboro*	36
	5.3.2 *Bar Harbor to Winter Harbor*	37
5.4	**Passenger Boat Selection and Description**	37
	5.4.1 *Monohull*	38
	5.4.2 *Catamaran*	39
5.5	**Service and Economic Parameters**	39
	5.5.1 *Seasonal service (commuter & recreational)*	41
	5.5.2 *Year round service (commuter & recreational)*	42
5.6	**Demand**	43
	5.6.1 *Commuters*	43
	5.6.2 *Recreational*	45
5.7	**Ferry Economic Model Results**	46
	5.7.1 *Seasonal service*	46
	5.7.2 *Year round*	47
	5.7.3 *Summary*	48
5.8	**Bus Service Links**	50
6	**Schoodic Bicycling Enhancement Options**	51
6.1	**Access and Use**	51
	6.1.1 *Current conditions and goals*	51
	6.1.2 *AASHTO guidelines*	52
	6.1.3 *Issues*	53
	6.1.4 *Integration with other projects and studies*	54

6.2 Demand   54

   6.2.1 Transportation Alternative 2   55

   6.2.2 Transportation Alternative 3   55

   6.2.3 Transportation Alternative 4   55

6.3 Schoodic Loop Road   55

   6.3.1 Current conditions and options   55

   6.3.2 One-way option   56

   6.3.3 Two-way option   56

   6.3.4 One way / two way option   56

   6.3.5 Two way / one way option   56

   6.3.6 Schoodic Loop Road   57

   6.3.7 Conclusion   57

6.4 Gouldsboro and Winter Harbor Roads   57

   6.4.1 Moore Road, Winter Harbor   57

   6.4.2 Route 186, Winter Harbor to Birch Harbor   57

   6.4.3 Schoodic Road, Gouldsboro   57

6.5 Park and Ride Opportunities   58

   6.5.1 Ferry service   58

   6.5.2 Bus and automobile   58

7   Bus Services   59

7.1 Bar Harbor to Schoodic Service   59

   7.1.1 Bus Only – Level One   60

   7.1.2 Bus Only – Level Two   61

7.2 Bus Links for Ferry Alternatives   63

   7.2.1 Bus /Ferry Links: Bar Harbor and Schoodic Peninsula   64

      7.2.1.1   Schoodic bus schedules   67

      7.2.1.2   Bar Harbor village shuttle   69

      7.2.1.3   Midday Bar Harbor – Acadia National Park bus link   69

7.3 Summary of Vehicle Requirements and Cost Projections   70

8   Transportation Alternatives Summary and Selection   71

8.1 Alternative 2   71

8.2 Alternative 3   71

8.3 Alternative 4   72

8.4 Selection   72

9   Schoodic Peninsula Roadway Impacts and Enhancements   75

9.1 Transportation Alternative 1   75

    9.1.1 Impacts   76

    9.1.2 Enhancements   77

9.2 Transportation Alternative 2   77

    9.2.1 Impacts   77

    9.2.2 Enhancements   78

9.3 Transportation Alternative 3   78

    9.3.1 Impacts   79

    9.3.2 Enhancements   79

9.4 Transportation Alternative 4   80

    9.4.1 Impacts   80

    9.4.2 Enhancements   81

9.5 Summary   81

10 Findings and Recommendations   83

10.1 Selection of Transportation Alternative   83

10.2 Ferry Services   84

10.3 Bicycle Transport Enhancements   85

10.4 Bus Service   86

10.5 Roadway Impacts and Enhancements   87

References   89

Figures

2-1   Map of Schoodic Peninsula   6

4-1   1990 Population Map, Hancock and Washington Counties   22
4-2   1990 Population Map, Journeys to Work in Bar Harbor   23

5-1   Schoodic Peninsula and Adjacent Waters   28
5-2   South Gouldsboro Dock   29
5-3   Winter Harbor Aerial Photograph   31
5-4   Winter Harbor Town Dock   31
5-5   Winter Harbor Marina Dock   33
5-6   Bar Harbor Aerial Photo   34
5-7   1 West Street Dock, Harbor Place Dock in Background   35
5-8   January – March Wind Data, 1998 – 2000   36
5-9   July – September Wind Data, 1998 – 2000   36
5-10 Net Income Summary for All Services   49
5-11 Revenue by Source for All Services   49

9-1   Roadway Traffic: Effect of Active Alternatives   82
          Relative to "No Action" Alternative

10-1 Net Annual Ferry Service Finances   85
10-2 Roadway Traffic: Effect of Active Alternatives   87
          Relative to "No Action" Alternative

Tables

4-1   Activities of Park Visitors   25

5-1   Particulars of Selected Boats   38
5-2   Ferry Economic and Operational Factors   40
5-3   Ferry Run Times   40
5-4   Summer Ferry Schedule, (1) Monohull   41
5-5   Daily Summer Service Run Time Summary   42
5-6   Winter Ferry Schedule, (1) Monohull   42
5-7   Daily Winter Service Run Time Summary   43
5-8   Average Daily Roundtrips, 1 Monohull, Seasonal   44
5-9   Average Daily Roundtrips, 1 Monohull, Off-Season   44
5-10   Average Daily Roundtrips, 1 Monohull, Yearly   44
5-11   One Monohull Ferry Service: Patronage for All Scenarios   45
5-12   Seasonal Service Finances, 50' Monohull   46
5-13   Seasonal Cost and Patronage Summary   47
5-14   Year Round Cost and Patronage Summary   48

6-1   Current Conditions of Roadway for Bicyclists   52
6-2   Alternative 3 Seasonal Bicycle Trips   55

7-1   Schedule - Level One Bus Service   60
7-2   Markets Served, Level One Bus Service   61
7-3   Schedule - Level Two Bus Service   61
7-4   Markets Served, Level Two Bus Service   63
7-5   Integrated Bar Harbor-Schoodic Bus and Ferry Schedule   66
7-6   Markets Served - Coordinated Bus and Ferry Schedules   67
7-7   Bar Harbor-Jackson Lab Village Shuttle Schedule   68
7-8   Summary of Vehicle Requirements and Cost Projections   70

9-1   Schoodic Area Vehicular Traffic   76

APPENDICES

A Draft Reuse Alternatives

B Ferry Financial Model

C Population and Employment Data and Forecasts

D Park Visitation Data and Forecasts

E Base Reuse Data and Forecasts

F Ferry Service Schedules, Demand and Patronage Data, Service Costs and Revenue

1   Introduction

1.1 Purpose of Report

This report supports Acadia National Park's ("the Park") development of an amendment to the 1991 General Management Plan (GMP) by identifying and assessing transportation alternatives to serve the Park's Schoodic Peninsula area. The amendment will be in response to the planned closure of several U.S. Navy facilities in and adjacent to the Park's Schoodic Peninsula lands and the potential resulting changes of use of that parkland. The Navy will return the Naval Security Group Activity ("the Navy base") at Schoodic Point land and facilities to the Park Service in June 2002 and the Park must identify base reuse alternatives and address the attendant transportation issues contiguous to and within the Schoodic parkland. This report addresses the transportation implications of the draft reuse concept alternatives provided by Acadia Park staff to the Volpe Center.

The focus of the transportation alternatives analysis will be ferry, bus, and bicycle modes to and within the Schoodic parkland, as well as an assessment of Schoodic area roadway impacts. The scope of the analysis includes external transport links to Mount Desert Island and transportation enhancements in and around the Schoodic parkland.

1.2 National Park Service Objectives

The mission objective of the Park Service is to protect the natural resources of the Schoodic parkland and to preserve its character as an un-crowded and quiet visitor experience. The specific objectives are to 1) identify Navy base reuse alternatives that are sensitive to local economic and political issues, and 2) provide for transportation needs of future visitors consistent with the mission objective for Schoodic.

The two specific objectives are clearly intertwined, since reuse of the base will imply certain transportation needs and may also affect visitation in the Schoodic parkland. This assessment must therefore include a picture of overall transportation needs for Schoodic Peninsula, including residents' commuter and other travel requirements.

1.3 Navy Base Closure

The Navy base closure includes the Schoodic Point base and other facilities. The most significant of the others is a substantial amount of single-family, duplex, and multi-family housing in Winter Harbor. There are also two large industrial and research buildings and a large antenna facility in Corea (a village in Gouldsboro).

1.3.1   Schoodic Point base

The Schoodic Point base is a campus complex of 90 acres and 50 buildings, including offices, residential units of various kinds, fire station, medical clinic, day care center, commissary, potable and waste water facilities, and numerous recreational assets put in place for use by Navy personnel. It includes buildings of historic value, campsites, a medical clinic, and a warehouse. The Navy plans to return the land and its facilities to the Park Service.

The Park Service has drafted three concept alternatives for the reuse of the base, all for a campus-style learning center sponsored by two or more public and private entities (e.g., Park Service, University of Maine, Bigelow Labs), each varying the center's size (both staff and facilities) and allowing for different visitor education opportunities (see Subchapter 2.2).

1.3.2 Winter Harbor Housing

The Navy housing in Winter Harbor consists of three separate complexes: 1) 20 single family houses known as Harbor View, situated north of the downtown area on Newman Street; 2) 14 duplexes (28 units) known as Ocean Heights situated just east of the downtown area off of Route 186; and 3) four apartment buildings totaling 32 units and several garage and storage buildings, known as Misty Harbor, located in the downtown area just behind the IGA grocery store.

The "Down East" communities, particularly Gouldsboro and Winter Harbor, have serious concerns about the economic and other community impacts of the base closure. At the peak manning levels in previously years, Navy personnel represented 500 people of the total Winter Harbor population of 900 and Navy operations provided substantial employment and business activity. There has been much public comment to the Park Service and in the various base closure fora that the reuse of the Schoodic Point base must replace, at least in part, that economic stimulus, as well as a serious concern expressed that the departure of the Navy will deplete public school populations and threaten the viability of the school district.

Any consideration of alternate transportation links to that area, particularly a ferry service, must account for several sources of patronage, including commuters to Mount Desert Island, traffic to and from the future facilities at the Navy base, and Park visitors seeking access to Schoodic Peninsula.

1.4 Park Service Alternative Transportation Program

The National Park Service has established that vehicle traffic in many national parks is equaling or exceeding capacity and has implemented a program to put alternatives in place. The benefits of alternative transport are clear: reduced road congestion and atmospheric pollution, improved visual and auditory values (i.e., fewer cars to see and hear), provision of an improved visitor experience, and more opportunities for resource interpretation

In the case of the Schoodic parkland of Acadia National Park, Park Service staff are in the process of establishing its "carrying capacity" through work currently underway by the University of Vermont School of Natural Resources. The Acadia GMP states that Schoodic is to retain its quiet character. The establishment of alternate transportation services to mitigate automobile traffic is intrinsically supportive of both the existing GMP and its forthcoming amendment dealing with the Navy base reuse.

1.5 Candidate Transportation Services

The Park Service desires an assessment of the MDI/Schoodic Peninsula link and the best transportation alternatives for reducing automobile traffic in the Schoodic parkland. Initial discussions with NPS staff led to the development of a work plan including consideration of ferry services, park and ride sites (car-to-, car-to-bus, and bus-to-), and local Schoodic "loop" bus service interface. This report also includes an assessment of roadway impacts within and adjacent to the Schoodic parkland, both with and without transportation alternatives in place.

1.6 Organization of Report

Chapter 2 describes the analytical approach adopted and the data inputs required to execute the analyses. Chapter 3 provides a general description of the project area. Chapter 4 presents the results of demographics, land use, and visitation data and projections. Chapters 5, 6, and 7 are the development and analysis of ferry, bicycle, and bus service modes. Chapter 8 summarizes the assessments of the transportation alternatives. Chapter 9 describes the projected impacts on Schoodic area roads, both without and with implementation of the alternate modes. Chapter 9 is the findings and recommendations.

2 Background

2.1 Description of Area

2.1.1 Acadia National Park

The following general description of the Park is derived from Park Service literature:

Acadia National Park was established 85 years ago and comprises 46,000 acres, mostly on Mount Desert Island on Maine's east coast, and including parkland on Schoodic Peninsula and many surrounding islands. The Park officially protects a large variety of plants, trees, and animals, the latter including 11 species of amphibians, 273 of birds, and four of fish. There are also many more species of terrestrial and marine mammals, including seals giving birth to their young. The Park is also a significant scientific and cultural education center for visitors of all ages.

Acadia Park provides visitors with a great variety of activities including sightseeing, hiking, camping, kayaking, canoeing, and bicycling. Guided tours on land and water help people understand the area and its biological importance. Popular sites and scenic areas include the Park Loop Road, Thunder Hole, Eagle Lake Carriage Road, Baker Island Light Station, Abbe Museum, Schoodic Peninsula and the Isle au Haut.

An important goal of the Park is to retain and restore its pristine condition, which aim is partially addressed through air quality monitoring for UV-b radiation, ozone, nitrous oxides, visibility, precipitation and other descriptors. Management of vehicular traffic is one measure for control of the levels of harmful pollutants.

Park staff must manage the conflicting needs of 1) providing myriad recreational and educational opportunities to millions of visitors and 2) maintaining and restoring a pristine condition to the fullest possible extent. The Schoodic peninsula parkland is subject to this dichotomy and its future transportation system particularly so since visitor impacts in the area are currently far less severe than on MDI.

2.1.2 Schoodic Peninsula

Schoodic Peninsula lies to the east of Mount Desert Island, separated by Frenchman Bay and a number of smaller islands. It is generally demarked by Maine Route 186 to the north connecting Winter Harbor and Birch Harbor, Frenchman Bay to the west, and the Gulf of Maine to the south and west. It makes up the southern portion of a larger mass of land projecting generally southward, or "down east", into the Gulf from U.S. Route 1 between the town of Sullivan and the border of Hancock and Washington Counties.

2.1.2.1   Parkland

The National Park owns most of the land on the southern end of Schoodic Peninsula, an area about 1.5 miles wide (east to west) and three miles long (north to south), in addition to four small islands in the adjacent waters. Big Moose Island is actually the southernmost part of the Peninsula and includes the scenic area at Schoodic Point and the Navy base. Visitors enjoy rocky shorelines, ocean vistas, and wooded uplands.

The park road provides access to visitors, most of whom travel through in private vehicles, and generally follows the shoreline except where it runs on the east side of the Navy base and Big Moose Island. Unimproved roads also provide access to the Schoodic Head, the highest point on the peninsula at 440' elevation, and to the ranger's residence. There is a limited number of hiking trails, one to Schoodic Head and another from Blueberry Hill, and many other walking opportunities along the shoreline.

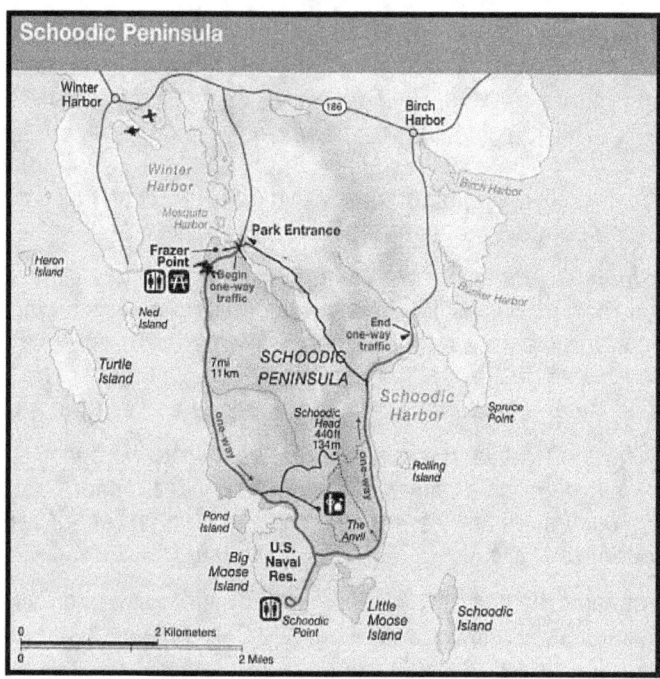

Source: National Park Service

Figure 2-1
Map of Schoodic Peninsula

2.1.2.2   Gouldsboro and Winter Harbor

The Town of Gouldsboro comprises the villages of West and South Gouldsboro, Birch Harbor Prospect Harbor, and Corea, covering the bulk of the landmass in and adjacent to Schoodic Peninsula. The 2000 Census reports that the Town's population is 1940.

The Town of Winter Harbor seceded from Gouldsboro in the late 1800s and is situated around the well protected harbor of the same name. Its downtown is the largest center of commercial activity in the area. Grindstone Neck, a small peninsula to the west of the harbor, is a residential area including many summer homes for seasonal residents. The 2000 Census reports that the Town's population is 990.

More detail on demographics and land use in these two towns appears in Chapter 4.

2.1.2.3   Navy base

The Naval Security Group Activity at Winter Harbor (the "base") makes up most of Big Moose Island, as seen in Figure 2-1. It now consists of 50 buildings and facilities, as described in subsection 1.3.1 and includes most of the northern, western, and southern shoreline of Big Moose Island. Access to the base is via the only stretch of two-way road within the Schoodic parkland, the spur leading from the one-way loop road to the Schoodic Point scenic area. Residents and visitors to the base must enter and exit the parkland on the one-way loop road.

2.1.2.4 Area roads

Primary road access to Schoodic Peninsula is from U.S. Route (USR) 1, connecting Ellsworth and points to the south, and Machias and points to the north. Interstate Highway Route 95 passes through Bangor approximately 35 miles north of Ellsworth; travelers on I95 take State Route (SR) 3 to Ellsworth, from where they can continue on SR 3 to MDI or take USR 1 north to the Schoodic region.

Access from Route 1 to Schoodic is via SR 186, a loop connecting twice with USR 1, or SR 195. SR 186 runs counterclockwise (south, then east, then north) through West Gouldsboro, South Gouldsboro, Winter Harbor, Birch Harbor, Prospect Harbor, and Gouldsboro. SR 195 leaves USR 1 between the two intersections of SR 186 and runs south directly to Prospect Harbor, where it ends at the intersection with SR 186.

The two local roads of interest for this study are Moore Road in Winter Harbor and Schoodic Road in Birch Harbor, which are used for ingress and egress to the park, respectively. These roads connect the park road to SR 186.

2.2 Reuse Alternatives

Park staff provided draft versions of three base reuse alternatives. While these may not represent the reuse alternatives in their final form, they served as a reasonable basis for the transportation alternatives analysis. The primary reuse purpose is that of a learning center, articulated in various intensities of use in the three alternatives. Summaries of the draft reuse alternatives appear below (full text in Appendix A).

2.2.1 Reuse Concept 1

Concept 1 is for a modest learning center, utilizing only the historic structures and facilities necessary for park support and the learning center and undertaking the most site restoration with no expansion of recreational facilities. The system of roads and paths would be reconfigured to create a more efficient and pleasant campus environment and the network of hiking trails connecting the base to Schoodic parkland around the perimeter of Big Moose Island would be opened to the public. Living accommodations would be available for up to 200 people and the learning center would have as many as 200 program users. The Schoodic parkland would support a moderate increase in visitor day use but have much less overnight use than did the base at its peak use by the Navy.

2.2.2 Reuse Concept 2

Concept 2 is for a more expansive research and education facility, to encompass science and education in natural and cultural conservation, and programs in natural and cultural history, conservation, science, music, and art. Facilities would include housing, food service, classrooms, archival collections storage, and laboratory space. The learning center would provide housing for 15-20 researchers and up to 100 students.

Accommodations would be available for up to a total of 300 people in campsites, apartments, and dormitories and the learning center would have as many as 500 program users daily. The Schoodic parkland would support a moderate increase in visitor day use, but it would have less overnight use than did the base at its peak use by the Navy.

2.2.3 Reuse Concept 3

Concept 3 expands the uses suggested in Concept 2, while retaining most of the existing Navy base buildings, leasing those not required for the learning center to compatible uses. The learning center would provide housing for 15-20 researchers and up to 190 students, with total accommodations available for up to 350 people in campsites, cabins, apartments, and dormitories. The learning center might have as many as 600 program users on site on a peak day. Leased office or research space might provide employment for an additional 50 people. The Schoodic unit of the park would experience a moderate increase in visitor day use, as well as overnight use.

3 Approach

3.1 General

The premises of the analysis are the 1) the mission objective of the Park Service to protect the natural resources of the Schoodic parkland, and 2) the provision for future transportation needs consistent with that mission objective and the identified Navy base reuse alternatives. It is also necessary to consider future transportation alternatives in light of all the needs of residents and non-Park visitors on the Peninsula. The transportation alternatives under consideration would consist of services owned and operated independent of the Park Service, mostly by private concerns, and would embrace all transportation markets in the area, not just Park visitors.

The approach in this report is therefore a thoroughgoing effort to characterize the project area, its demographics, land use and growth trends, current transportation services, trip-to-work and other transportation needs (with consideration of the Navy properties' reuses), and the projected visitors' needs in Acadia National Park. Site visits, stakeholder interviews, and data acquisition efforts were all carried out with this broad viewpoint in mind. The analyses which follow likewise encompass the entire breadth of local transportation markets.

3.2 Transportation Alternatives

The Transportation Alternatives considered, by direction of the Park Service, are itinerant scheduled services and opportunities such as park-and-ride presented to visitors and the public as a whole to leave their cars and proceed by their own chosen mode (i.e., on or foot, kayak or canoe). The focus of the study is ferry and/or bus service from MDI to Schoodic Peninsula, park-and-ride opportunities on Schoodic, and attendant local bus links among MDI service terminuses, local residential areas, and recreational destinations both within the Schoodic parkland and the neighboring towns.

The development and characterization of the Alternatives are set at future dates when the Navy base reuse has been implemented and reflect future demand projections. The dates chosen for the analysis bracket a "look" period from 2005 to 2015. The year 2005 is seen as a realistic start point where the Navy base reuse and development of proposed transportation infrastructure elements will be fully realized. The 2015 endpoint matches the time frame under consideration in the GMP amendment. All financial elements of the analysis are expressed in year 2001 dollars, however, for consistency and simplicity.

The Alternatives are integrated among the transport modes considered, i.e., route and schedule considerations among ferry, bus, and other modes dovetail to provide the best conceptual intermodal transfers. The demand and market aspects of each Alternative are therefore integrated analytically; the results reflect "organic" wholes rather than separate pieces of the system.

The Transportation Alternatives chosen are the result of the project team's observations of the project area and its needs, practical considerations relating to the identified candidate transport modes, and direction of the Park Service. They are:

> ➢ *Alternative 1* – No action.

> ➤ **Alternative 2** – No ferry service, substituted by year round commuter bus service, bus service commuter links in Bar Harbor and on Schoodic Peninsula, park-and-ride facility in Winter Harbor, and circle bus route on Schoodic Peninsula connecting park-and-ride users to destinations in the Schoodic parkland and nearby towns.

> ➤ **Alternative 3** – Seasonal ferry service (May - October) for commuter and recreational users, bus service commuter links in Bar Harbor and on Schoodic Peninsula, circle bus route on Schoodic Peninsula connecting recreational ferry passengers to destinations in the Schoodic parkland and nearby towns, winter commuter bus service and backup for ferry cancellations, and park-and-ride facility in Winter Harbor.

> ➤ **Alternative 4** – Year round ferry service for commuter and recreational users, bus service commuter links in Bar Harbor and on Schoodic Peninsula, circle bus route on Schoodic Peninsula connecting recreational ferry passengers to destinations in the Schoodic parkland and nearby towns, backup commuter bus service for ferry cancellations due to weather or operational problems, and park-and-ride facility in Winter Harbor.

Alternatives 2, 3, and 4 are hitherto collectively referred to as the "active" Alternatives. The discussion following presents the approaches taken to characterization of the individual modes.

3.2.1 Ferry services

The idea of a ferry across Frenchman Bay connecting Bar Harbor to Schoodic Peninsula is not new and indeed is a geographically obvious concept. Ferries in the past provided vital transportation links both within the area and to greater New England. These services faded in the post-war period with the automobile's rise to primacy, as did ferry services nationwide. The recent renewal of public interest in ferries and waterborne transportation in general has manifested itself locally in the appearance of a number of ferry and excursion services, including a Bar Harbor to Winter Harbor ferry which has operated during the summers of 2000 and 2001 (the "Bar Harbor Ferry").

The ferry services identified for this study are not similar in their particulars to any past or currently existing service. The boats and schedules employed meet the specific needs and market demand foreseen, in particular, the speed of the boats and frequency of service.

3.2.1.1   Commuter and recreational markets

All potential markets are considered as potential sources of patronage for a new ferry service. The demand values in the commuter and recreational markets (in both directions) are separately calculated; however, the ferry patronage for the various scenarios considered is taken as the total of the two and modeled "organically" (demand calculations methodology appears in Section 3.3). The two services modeled will be year-round and seasonal, the latter taken as the six months from the beginning of May through the end of October.

3.2.1.2   Vessel selection

Candidate boats for the modeled services were selected after discussions with local operators, consideration of local needs and conditions, and investigating available ferry data bases, notably "Ferry Lines of the United States", developed by the Volpe Center in 2000 for the Federal Highway Administration to meet a mandate of the Transportation Equity Act for the 21st Century (TEA 21). The project team selected catamaran and monohull boats with a minimum speed requirement of 18 knots to provide headway (service frequency) times of 80 minutes or less.

3.2.1.3   Terminals

The project team identified candidate ferry terminal sites both in Bar Harbor and on Schoodic Peninsula, with the insight of Park Service representatives and local stakeholders. The sites were all visited by Volpe Center representatives and assessed for physical condition, automobile access, parking, navigational aspects, and local use patterns.

3.2.1.4   Ferry Service Cost and Revenue Model

The Volpe Center developed a ferry service cost and revenue model for the U.S Navy Office of Naval Research (ONR) while preparing a study on the commercial viability of the SLICE, a high speed, multi-hull displacement craft developed by Lockheed, similar to "small waterplane area, twin hull" (SWATH) now in use as research vessels and in some commercial passenger services (Volpe Center, 2001). The report for ONR included eight U.S. regional market case studies comparing SLICE to other high speed craft. The ferry model has since been refined and modified for use in several commercial passenger service studies by the Volpe Center, including Park Service ATP projects for the Boston Harbor Islands National Park Area, New York Gateway Parks and Fire Island National Seashore.

The model evaluates the relative economic performance of the various ferry route and service alternatives proposed herein. The financial performance in each case is expressed by yearly net income or loss (the model also calculates internal rate of return on the required equity investment over the estimated vessel service life). The financial analysis applies to a broad spectrum of ferry operations, including cases with government subsidies, where minimizing the subsidy needed to produce neutral or positive return on equity investment is an appropriate measure.

In keeping with generally accepted principals and methods for the financial analysis of transportation business entities, total expenses (cash outflows) are classified into the three mutually exclusive categories of *vessel debt repayment, direct operating costs* and *indirect operating costs*. Vessel debt repayment includes principal and interest payments on the portion of the vessel purchase price not funded by the equity investment of the owners (20% down payment and 15 year term assumed). It is assumed that debt service continues for the owner through 2015.

Direct operating costs for the vessel include crew costs (in these cases, deck crew only, excluding passenger service crew), fuel and lubricant costs, hull insurance, and vessel maintenance (maintenance costs rise with vessel age and ten years is added to the ages of the candidate boats in the 2015 scenarios). Indirect operating costs include terminal related costs such as passenger facility charges, protection and indemnity insurance, docking fees, marketing and advertising, and general administration.

In evaluating vessel attributes that affect operator financial performance (e.g., fuel consumption, vessel maintenance, vessel purchase price, etc.), historically observed data were obtained whenever possible from sources such as the current operators of the vessel(s) or operators of similar vessel(s), or vessel designers and shipyards.

A complete and detailed description of the ferry financial model appears in Appendix B.

3.3 Travel Demand Analysis

The analysis generally must address a number of potential markets in the future, all of which together are necessary for the economic and political success of any new transportation service. Those markets are characterized overall as recreational and commuter users, whose specific elements include the following:

- Acadia National Park visitors traveling between MDI and Schoodic for recreational purposes.

- Commuters traveling from the Schoodic region to jobs at Jackson Laboratory and elsewhere in Bar Harbor and reverse commuters traveling from Bar Harbor to jobs in Schoodic Peninsula, including those projected for new activities at the Navy base.
- Acadia National Park staff, staff from the future activities at the Navy base, guests and researchers at the Navy base, and other visitors traveling between Bar Harbor and Schoodic Peninsula for both business and pleasure.

3.3.1 Overview of data resources

The travel demand model set used in this study was developed from several data sources in order to help identify patterns of trip making between Mount Desert Island and the Schoodic Peninsula. They consist of demographic data, namely, population and employment data, National Park Service research on visitation and park use, several independent surveys and reports, and field work by the project team. The study area that this data was collected for was the Down East and Acadia Region of Maine, including Hancock and Washington Counties.

The look period and scenario forecast years were determined by three criteria:

- Current conditions scenario – the year 2000, chosen particularly because of newly available descriptive data from the census.
- Short- term forecast year – the year 2005, representative of the realistic completion of build out for the Navy base reuse concepts.
- Horizon year – 2015, as compatible with the vision of the Acadia Park General Management Plan amendment, and providing for a long-term perspective.

3.3.1.1 Population

The population data came from two sources, the 2000 Census and the Hancock County Planning Commission (HCPC). The population data helped to determine the distribution of individuals by community in the study area and identify sources of possible recreational trip making activity. The 2000 Census was checked against the 1998 Hancock County Data to determine consistency, and the data then broken down into several groups by age. The breakdown helped to identify market segments and the effects of changes in land use or transportation services and was structured as follows: children younger than 12 years old and 12 to 18 years old, senior citizens, and the remaining population.

Population forecasts for 2005 and 2015 were obtained from the University of Southern Maine (USM), Center for Business and Economic Research, developed for use in the 2000 Long Range Employment and Population Forecasts for the State of Maine (Colgan, 2000). Those forecasts, originally developed only for counties and groups of counties, were adjusted to the 2000 Census estimates by changing the model's estimates of economic migration. The 2005 and 2015 forecasted populations for individual towns in the study area were obtained by assuming that they would have similar and proportional distributions as the 2000 Census totals (detailed population data and forecasts appear in Appendix C).

3.3.1.2   Employment and journey to work data

There were three sources for employment data: the 1997 Economic Census, 1990 journey-to-work Census data, and Employment Profiles from the HCPC. These data identified areas generating and attracting work trips in the study area and were the basis for a database of current and future commuter trips between Mount Desert Island and the Schoodic Peninsula. The 1997 Economic Census and the HCPC provided data by sectors for year round employment. HCPC employment data characterized seasonal employment by the retail, hotel, and restaurant segments of the workforce. A 1996 HCPC commuter survey, conducted for a Schoodic - Bar Harbor ferry study, and the 1990 Census journey-to-work data (2000 Census data not available for this report) were the basis for determination of commuter demand and distribution. The commuter survey provided insight as to the major employers and the attitudes of their employees towards a new ferry service. It was assumed that commuters would work 260 days a year.

Employment forecasts for 2005 and 2015 were also obtained from USM, which updated 1997 employment data for each region to 1998 and 1999 using the Maine Department of Labor data on wage and salary employment. The employment concept used in these forecasts is "total employment", which combines wage and salary employment, with estimates of self-employment and farm employment. The employment figures are thus noticeably higher than those published by the Maine Department of Labor.

The differences in forecasting concepts necessitated an estimating technique for the 1998 employment update which adjusts the change in total employment in each region and industry by the growth rate in wage and salary employment as measured by the Maine Department of Labor (MDOL). For 1999, monthly MDOL data from the *Labor Market Digest* is published for the state and for the Portland and Lewiston Metropolitan Statistical Areas. Growth rates for each industry in these two regions were used to estimate future growth. Statewide growth rates for 1999 for each industry were then distributed to other regions (Hancock and Washington Counties were taken together) based on each industry and region's share of 1998 growth rates. The Hancock and Washington Counties employment projections for 2005 and 2015 are also identical to the USM estimates.

Conversion of future county employment to future community employment was by allocation of shares of employment proportionally among the towns in the study area based on the 1998 employment distribution in the Economic Census. The new employment forecasts by community were the basis of local residence and journey-to-work profiles, using the same distribution as the 1990 trip flows.

It was assumed that the all of the commuters who worked on the Navy base in 1990 resided in Winter Harbor and this employment was assumed to be reduced by 50% in order to calculate the 2000 journey-to-work trip flows. The forecast years had the employment for the Navy base in Winter Harbor removed prior to proportionally distributing the employment across communities in the study area. After this distribution occurred, employment estimates from the conceptual plans were added to Winter Harbor and distributed using the distribution of adult population in the study area. Detailed employment data and forecasts appear in Appendix C.

3.3.1.3   National Park visitation and survey data

The NPS and the HCPC provided data and surveys on use, views, characteristics, and preferences of the visitors in and around the National Park. These data were instrumental in determining the magnitude and distribution of recreational trips in Acadia and Schoodic. The visitation data were derived from official NPS tabulations for every year and month between 1990 and 2000. The ten-year time period showed important seasonal trends.

A 1998 visitor study provided data on visitor destinations, transport modes, party sizes, and preferences for places and events. The 1996 HCPC ferry service survey provided insight into what factors relating to ferry service were important to the tourists. The Park Service conducted a survey on the use of the Island Explorer Bus System in the summer of 1999. The Island Explorer is the primary public transit option on Mt Desert Island; it provides a basis for understanding who might be utilize other transport alternatives and why. The project team also examined preliminary research by the University of Vermont from the summer of 2000 investigating park use and issues relating to carrying capacity.

In 1999, Acadia Park staff developed an estimate of visitation growth rates for park recreational visits using data gathered between 1990 and 1998. The resulting average growth rate of 1.26% is the basis for projected visitations for 2005 and 2015, starting with actual year 2000 visitation data. The projected monthly and daily visitation are based on the same variations seen between 1990 and 2000. It was assumed that the daily recreational trips could occur on any day of the week, 360 days a year, but they would be function of the monthly variation that the NPS has observed over the last 10 years. Detailed visitation data and forecasts appear in Appendix D.

3.3.1.4   Base reuse analysis

The Schoodic Navy base reuse is a significant element of future employment, visitation, and journey-to-work calculations. The characterization and quantification of these activities are based on several conditions and assumptions. The bases of the analysis are traffic data from the Park Service on the historical trip-making activity at the base (between from 1990—full operation—and 2000—partial operation of about 50%) and the three conceptual plans developed by the Park Service, each one representing a different intensity level of base reuse. Concept 1 is the "Low" or minimum build out scenario, while Concept is the "High" or maximum build out scenario.

For the purpose of this study, 2005 was considered the earliest timeframe that the Reuse Concepts could be implemented. The analysis includes the high and low buildout scenarios for each year and consideration of three time frames each. The seasonal time frame includes the six months of May through October, and the year round cases include January through December. The daily demand was calculated as an average of weekday and weekend use for the seasonal and year round cases.

Each of the park's conceptual plans identifies buildings to be retained and their uses. Examination of each building and use is the basis of commuter and recreational trip-making activities, resulting in numbers of individuals traveling, types of trip, and numbers of trips. Park personnel, teachers, researchers, and retail operators were considered commuters (with seasonal fluctuation) because they would have a regular work schedule on the base. All non-regular visitors to the base qualify as recreational trips, including purely recreational visitors, students, and users of the meeting rooms (even if present for purposes of work). Detailed base reuse data and forecasts appear in Appendix E.

3.3.2   Demand modeling process

Travel demand calculations are by the commonly applied four step modeling process for transportation planning, originally developed in the 1970s by the Federal Highway Administration for use by municipal planning organizations. The four steps are: trip generation, trip distribution, model split, and assignment. The process combines socio-economic data and characteristics of the transportation system to predict trip flows between different geographic areas, in this study towns on Mount Desert Island and in Hancock and Washington Counties. The transportation systems of interest are described by the four identified transportation alternatives in the years 2000 (baseline only), 2005, and 2015. These systems can include but are not limited to roadways, ferries, bus routes, bicycle routes, and walking trails. The socio-economic and demographic input factors predict the distribution of trip flows between Mount Desert Island and the Schoodic Peninsula, varied for the three Base reuse concepts.

3.3.2.1   Trip generation

Trip generation is the first sub-model of the conventional four-step model sequence and predicts the number of trips generated at and attracted to a given location, based on all persons who could possibly use any mode of transportation. The towns identify the beginning and end points of the trips flows but not where they come from or where they go once they leave the town. The trips generated are based on the socio-economic characteristics of the study area population, specifically, commuter and recreational trips. The trips generated by the base reuse were broken down into commuters and recreational trips as well. The basis for commuter trips is journey-to-work totals, economic census, and the reuse plans and that for recreational trips is population data, park visitation numbers, and base reuse plans.

3.3.2.2   Trip distribution

Trip distribution (defined by the variables "i j") is the second step and it links the trip origins and destinations. In this case, the trip distribution model predicts how many of the trips originating in town i will terminate in town j. The distribution for work trips in this study was derived from Census journey-to-work data for 1990. Because of the lack of 2000 journey-to-work data, it was assumed that the 2000, 2005, and 2015 distribution of trips would not be significantly different from that of 1990 with the exception of the trip patterns due to the base reuse.

Recreational trips were distributed based on the survey and visitation data. Recreational and commuter trips generated by the base reuse were distributed to the towns in the study area proportionally based on their population and employment. This phase identifies the number of trips, also called the demand, between Mount Desert Island and the Schoodic Peninsula. Once the demand was identified, the markets for a new ferry service needed to be determined. This was done by looking at travel times between all of the communities in the study area using the current transportation system and the proposed transportation system that included a ferry and supplemental bus services.

3.3.2.3   Model split

Model spilt, or mode choice, is the third step in the modeling process and predicts how the demand between Mount Desert Island and Schoodic Peninsula will break down, by mode of transportation. Data from reports by the HCPC and survey data from the Island Explorer Study were the basis of an estimated 7% to 8% of people who would be likely to switch from the dominant transport mode (automobile) to an alternative mode such as a ferry or a bus. "Elasticities" determine changes in ridership within or between transit modes due to variations in service characteristics such as price, run-time, and headway (frequency of service). As an example, an elasticity of –0.40 means that for every 10% increase in run time a 4% reduction in ridership could be expected. The elasticities used here are based on research by the Federal Highway Administration in several areas in the United States over the last 20 years.

3.3.2.4   Assignment

The last step assigns people to various combinations of transportation modes (e.g., vehicle, ferry, bus) and routes. This was done for each year, ferry option, alternative, and time frame that was considered. Auto occupancies based on trip purpose were used to create vehicle trips. The vehicle trips were manually assigned to the roadway based on the shortest observable path.

3.4 Demand for Ferry Service

3.4.1 Data resources

The demand for the ferry service was calculated using the four step process described above. The demand for three ferry services, both seasonal and year round, was identified by commuter and recreational trips, including trips from the base reuse options. The analysis includes the high and low reuse scenarios for each year of interest (2000, 2005, and 2015). The seasonal use factored in seasonal employment based on HCPC research.

Recreational trips were incorporated based on current and projected visitation data from the NPS. Using survey data from the NPS, it was assumed that the recreational trips would be derived from three sources.

- 11% of the total projected visitors to Acadia National Park would visit the Schoodic Peninsula (1998 Visitor Survey results).
- 5% of the inhabitants of Schoodic Peninsula would take annual recreational visits to Mount Desert Island (Institute of Transportation Engineers, 1993).
- Recreational trips generated by the high and low base reuse scenarios.

3.4.2 Modeling process

The calculation of total trip generation and trip distribution among communities (demand) preceded the definition of the market area for commuters and recreational riders that might use the ferry service. For commuters, this was based initially on travel times between the communities and a rough assessment of the travel time-savings benefit for each community. The market area for the ferry service on Mount Desert Island was determined to be the communities of Bar Harbor and Mount Desert, because of the location of the dock in Bar Harbor and the limited transit options to or from other communities on the island. The market area on Schoodic Peninsula consisted of all the towns in Hancock and Washington Counties east of Sorrento, based on travel times to the dock, wait time, run-time, and a terminal time to access their final destination. The wait time was a function of the headway for each ferry option. The run time was the total time it took to go from the dock in Winter Harbor to departing the boat in Bar Harbor. The terminal time was an average time to get to locations in Bar Harbor or Desert Island.

The market area for recreational trips was developed more narrowly. Survey data indicate that Mount Desert Island will provide virtually all demand for Schoodic Peninsula. Recreational trips from Schoodic Peninsula to Mount Desert Island were assumed to originate from either Winter Harbor or Gouldsboro and be destined to Bar Harbor.

Determination of the mode splits for the market areas was the next step. Research has shown that people pick public forms of transit over the automobile about 8% of the time, which proportion was the basis for average demand for new ferry services for commuter and recreational use. Comparison of different ferry services (candidate boats) was by the two key service characteristics of run time and headway. An average run-time and headway was calculated for the three services and this was assumed to represent the demand that was derived from mode split. To differentiate the changes in ridership between the ferry services, an elasticity of −0.3 was used for the run time and −0.4 for the headway for seasonal use. Park Service research and data on off-season use were the basis of off-season elasticity factors. These were added together to create yearly use.

The mode assignment had several results: 1) origin and destinations of travelers by given transportation modes; 2) determination whether adequate parking spaces are available at proposed terminals to encourage use of a particular mode; 3) identification from survey data of levels of use; and 4) identification of the impacts to the local roadway system. Attributing an auto occupancy based on the nature of the trip to the commuters and recreational users of the ferry determined the number of vehicles that were changing paths. These vehicles were then added to the roadways by manually determining the path that they would have most likely used.

3.5 Bicycleway Enhancements & Usage

3.5.1 Data resources and analysis

The determination of current usage and future enhancement opportunities in and around Schoodic Peninsula was straightforward. Current usage for commuters derives from 1990 Census Mode of Transportation to Work data. The result was a very low number which probably shows only those commuting within their own town. It was assumed that none of the commuters in the forecast years would use bicycles to access the ferry.

The 1998 Summer Visitor Survey provides more current data on recreational use. Approximately 36% of all Park visitors on MDI use bicycles in some way. The University of Vermont's summer 2000 study showed that 17% of the people visiting the Schoodic Peninsula parkland used bicycles. Since Schoodic lacks the attraction of the carriage road system on Mount Desert Island, it is unlikely that use on Schoodic there will approach that of MDI. Since alternative transportation options and infrastructure improvements can be expected to increase use, the midpoint between the two currently reported values was chosen as to represent the projected upper level of use. Therefore, a range of 17% - 26% of projected recreational trips to Schoodic Peninsula are assumed to be on s.

3.5.2 Park and ride assessment

The availability of one or more park-and-ride lots on Schoodic would provide the opportunity for people to park cars outside the parkland and then go biking or paddling. Two candidate lots near the chosen ferry terminal are the subject of analysis of commuter use and recreational use. Both of these lots would have access to the proposed bus loop service going around Schoodic Peninsula.

Recreational park-and-ride use is a function of total recreational visits to the Schoodic Peninsula, calculated by applying 17% - 26% to the total recreational demand. The same percentage determines the number of people bringing s to Schoodic on the ferry. users arriving by ferry are subtracted from the total number to determine the number of users arriving by automobile and using park-and-ride facilities. Survey data on auto occupancies assigns bicyclists to a found number of vehicles, which are then assigned to the roadways and park-and-ride lots.

3.6 Analysis of Roadway Traffic

3.6.1 Data resources

The traffic impacts were examined for each alternative, year, and time frame based on the assignment process. The roadways that were examined are Moore Road (Schoodic parkland entrance), Wonsqueak Road (Schoodic parkland exit), and SR 186 in Winter Harbor and Gouldsboro. Traffic data from the HCPC and the State of Maine provide details into the base year 2000 traffic volumes. This was supplemented by fieldwork to determine traffic patterns and operating speeds on the roadways.

3.6.2 Analysis

Transportation Alternatives 2, 3 and 4 will be compared with Alternative 1 for each year and time frame to determine numerical traffic impacts, expressed as average daily traffic (ADT). The ADT for each roadway will be related to its theoretical maximum carrying capacity to produce the value "volume-to-capacity" (V/C). The maximum carrying capacity of a roadway is based on the width, speed limit, shoulders, terrain, surrounding land use, types, and numbers of vehicles using it. As the V/C ratio approaches 1.0, the effectiveness of the roadway to carry those vehicles decreases. This quantifies levels of congestion in a relative manner for a particular roadway. It is assumed for these purposes that V/C represents the roadway's use and performance over a 12 hour period each day. This index usually quantifies peak hour performance, but because of the lack of data at this temporal scale, the roads can be compared only on a daily (12 hour) basis for each combination of Transportation Alternative and Reuse Concept.

3.7 Bus Services

Inter-regional (between Bar Harbor and Schoodic Peninsula) and local (both for Bar Harbor and Schoodic) bus service concepts were developed as integral elements of the Transportation Alternatives and, in particular, coordinated with the ferry schedules developed for Alternatives 3 and 4. Each is the product of a transportation planning consultant based in Bar Harbor with extensive experience with the local bus services.

Chapter 7 also includes a demand analysis for these bus services whose basis is the same as that earlier described for ferry services, with appropriate adjustments of trip and headway times, fares, and their associated elasticities.

4 Demographics, Land Use, and Park Visitation

4.1 Demographics

Past and current demographics and growth projections in and around Schoodic Peninsula comprise a critical element of the transportation model and analysis. The two key components of the demographics are the geographic distributions of population and employment.

4.1.1 Population

The population in Hancock County was approximately 51,580 in the year 2000, distributed among 37 different communities, with a low of 40 persons in living in Frenchboro and a high of 6,460 people in Ellsworth. Hancock County saw an annual population growth rate of 7% in the 1990s. The Maine Department of Human Services projects that Hancock County's population will increase by 10.5% during the next decade; much faster than the 6.3% projected statewide increase. Washington County had a population of approximately 33,770 in the year 2000. This was distributed among 48 communities, with a low of 20 in Codyville and had a high of 2,350 in Calais and represented a slight decline in growth during the 1990's. Figure 4-1 depicts local population distribution based on data available from the 1990 Census.

The highest growth during the last decade was in the coastal areas in both counties and is a trend expected to continue into the forecast years, with the highest growth occurring in Hancock County. The coastal areas also experience a large seasonal increase of population during the summer months

Winter Harbor and Gouldsboro had populations of 990 and 1,940, respectively, in the year 2000. Navy base personnel accounted for about 500 people living in Winter Harbor in military housing at its peak use. The population with dependents has declined steeply as the Navy has phased out use of the base by many of its tenants and functions. Based on the USM forecasts for Hancock and Washington Counties for 2005, Winter Harbor and Gouldsboro are expected to see their population increase slightly. This trend is expected to continue through 2015.

Coastal towns in Washington County east of Schoodic include Stueben, Cherryfield, and Milbridge. They all have a populations in the range of 1,100 to 1,300 with Milbridge being the largest. Growth there is expected to be lower than in Hancock County's coastal towns.

4.1.2 Employment

Year round employment in Hancock County was approximately 34,400 in 1998, Ellsworth and Bar Harbor the leading employment sites with 9,800 and 6,900 respectively. The fastest growing segments of this work force were reported to be the service sector and the self-employed. Hancock County also had a seasonal work force of 2,700 in the year 2000, mostly in the retail, hotel, and food services (ref HCPC Website). Summer employment can account for 75% of the total workers in these sectors. During the 1990s, Hancock County saw a significant increase in year round and seasonal employment. This trend is expected to continue, especially in coastal areas with good access to the transportation system.

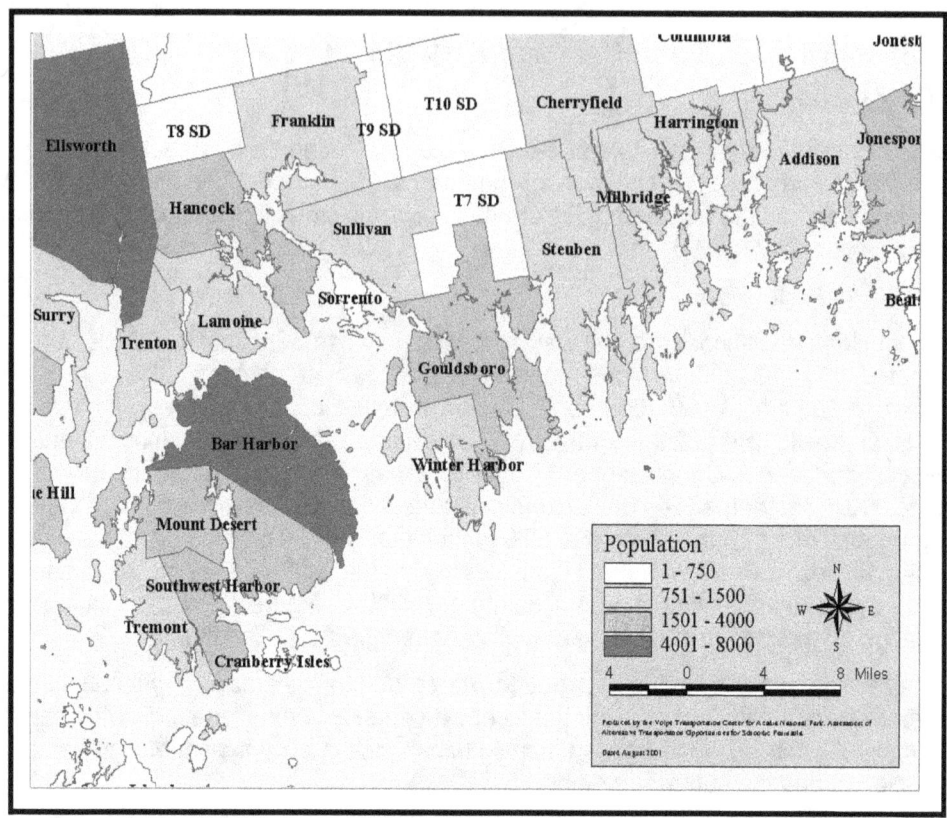

Source of data: 1990 U.S. Census, GIS data from State of Maine

Figure 4-1
1990 Population Map, Hancock and Washington Counties

Washington County had 19,100 year round jobs in 1998 led by Machias with over 3,700. Several inland communities had no employment. Washington County's coastal communities each provide between 140 and 930 jobs. The forecasts show that Washington County will see modest gains in year round employment, mainly along the coast.

Winter Harbor had an employment base of 460 individuals in 1998. The base closing will ultimately reduce this number by 200 to 300 military and civilian jobs. Gouldsboro had an employment base of approximately of 590 jobs, a number expected to decline slightly with the closures of the Schoodic base and the Corea radar installation. The Conceptual Plans provide for a portion of the jobs lost due to the base closing to be replaced in future years. The Volpe Center assessed the building use scenarios in the draft reuse concepts prepared by the Park and estimates that Concept 1 ("Low Reuse" Concept) will provide 70 jobs and that Concept 2 ("High Reuse" Concept) will provide 160 jobs; these numbers are held constant in the years 2005 & 2015.

Bar Harbor is the second largest provider of jobs in the summer and in the winter months. Several of the largest employers in this area are located here. They include Jackson Labs with over 1,000 employees, the College of the Atlantic and MDI Labs.

Bar Harbor also has a large number of seasonal workers, of course. Because of the lack of affordable housing on Mount Desert Island, a number of these workers commute from towns more than 20 miles away, proportional to the numbers of year round workers in those towns. Bar Harbor summer employment can increase by up to 2,000 (totaling 2,700) to cater to seasonal trade demands. Employment growth in Bar Harbor has been and will continue to be heavily influenced by recreational visitation to Acadia National Park, which is expected to see steady growth.

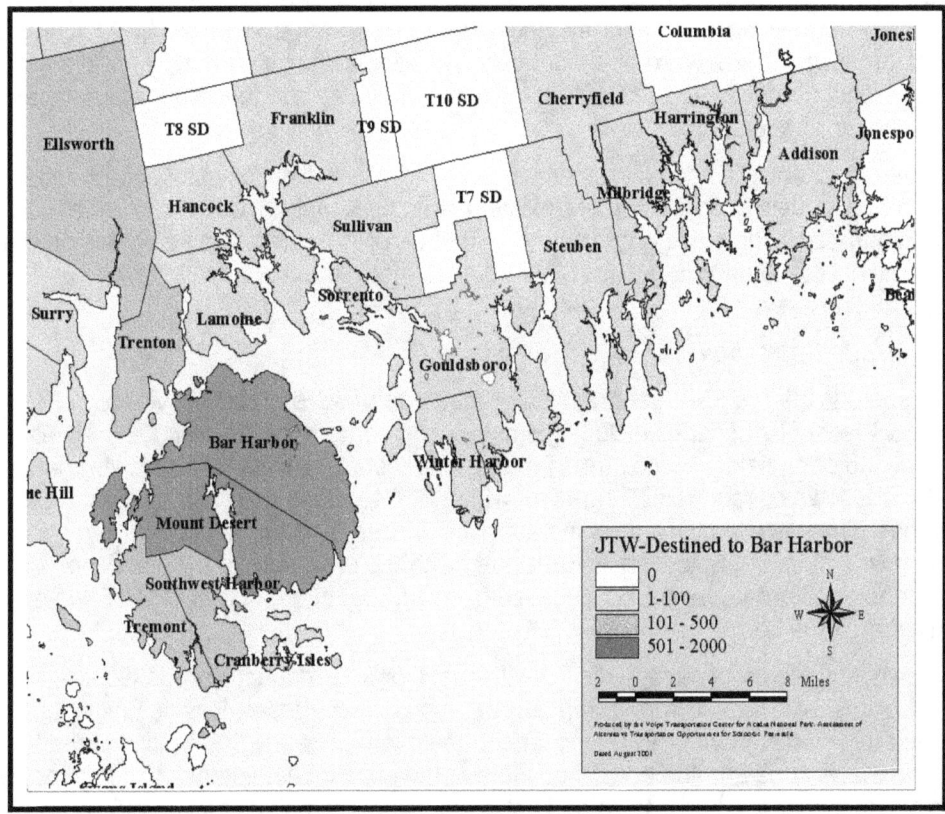

Source of data: 1990 U.S. Census, GIS data from State of Maine

<u>**Figure 4-2**</u>
1990 Population Map, Journeys to Work in Bar Harbor

4.2 Land Use

Characterization of an area's land use brings an understanding of the setting in which population and employment comparisons are made and provides insight into the type of structures the population is living in, their density, the surrounding environment, and work place descriptors.

4.2.1 Winter Harbor

Winter Harbor traditionally has been a fishing village with some commercial shipping of lumber in its early days. According to the Town's last Comprehensive Growth Plan (1994), the town covers 8,031 acres, 38% of which is tree growth. The town also has an extensive wetlands system. There has been limited farming and no known mining activity. The largest tract of undeveloped land is owned by Acadia National Park. Other tracts are held by private and corporate entities and the majority of them have access to the local road system (Town of Winter Harbor, 1994).

In the last 20 years, very little new housing or roads have been built with the exception of the military housing units. The military housing can be divided up into 3 groups, officer housing, military apartments, and military owned duplexes. Most new private residential construction has been in the Deep Cove area, along Summer Harbor Road, and along Hillcrest Drive. Other new housing units exist but they are few and scattered across the town. There were approximately 200 year round single-family homes and 120 seasonal homes in 1994. Overall, residential housing accounted for approximately 6% of the land cover in the town.

Commercial structures account for less than 2% of the land cover. Most of the retail and service industries operate in pre-existing structures that have historically been used for that purpose. There are approximately 80 structures in town that serve this purpose. Several local roads and State Rte (SR) 186 account for the majority of the transportation system.

4.2.2 Gouldsboro

Gouldsboro is a large town geographically, made up of several distinct villages offering a wide variety of landscapes including small village centers, harbors and shorelines, forests, and open fields. According to the Town's last Comprehensive Growth Plan (1993), the town covers 51,519 acres, of which 22,045 acres are bodies of water or wetlands. There are significant fishing activities, limited farming, and no current mining in the town. Most of the town is undeveloped with the exception of the coastline. Many interior portions are undeveloped because of limited transportation access (Town of Gouldsboro, 1993).

The town is made up of several distinct villages; Corea, Prospect Harbor, South Gouldsboro, West Gouldsboro, Birch harbor, and Bunker Harbor. Residential units account for the majority of developed land in the town, at nearly 5%. This is spread out through the villages and the coastline. Commercial and industrial units account for less than 1% of the land cover in town and are primarily located along the waterfront. The town has several key roads (USR 1, SR 186, and SR195) as well as local roads.

4.3 Park Use

Research on visitation to and use of Acadia National Park has historically focused on Mount Desert Island, and Schoodic Peninsula has only recently been the subject of systematic data collection. Visitation in the Park overall has increased gradually over the last ten years and leveled off in the last two years. Recreational visits to Acadia in the year 2000 numbered 2.47 million. "High" season is June through August, August being the busiest with 595,000 visitors. The shoulder months of May and October saw 166,000 and 253,000 visitors, respectively. Visitation drops off markedly outside of the peak and shoulder months.

Based on the 1.26% annual growth rate, the Park is expected to see an increase of 160,000 recreational visits for a total of 2.63 million in 2005. Projected visitation in the year 2015 is 510,000 more people than in the year 2000, a total of 3.14 million. T1he majority of the growth will likely occur between May and October.

Surveys conducted on Mount Desert Island and on Schoodic Peninsula over the last three years give a good understanding of Park visitor activities currently and those they are likely to choose in the future (Table 4-1). Scenic drives are the most common activity in both areas, with similarly high proportions. Hiking and walking are chosen far more often on MDI than at Schoodic, a fact easily explained by MDI's extensive trail system contrasting to the limited opportunities at Schoodic. There is significant boating and kayaking activity MDI, but these data are currently lacking for Schoodic. Recreational trip making activities tend to peak in the midday, between 10:00 am and 2:00 pm. The midday peak is more pronounced on Schoodic Peninsula because of its relatively remote location.

Activity by Visitors	Mount Desert Island	Schoodic Peninsula
Scenic drive	86%	81%
Hike on trails	72%	33%
Walk	40%	27%
Bicycle	36%	17%
Boat on lakes	13%	No data
Kayak	11%	No data
Mount Desert Island data from summer of 1998		
Schoodic data from summer of 2000		

Sources: Littlejohn, 1999; University of Vermont, 2000.

Table 4-1
Activities of Park Visitors

5 FERRY SERVICE

This chapter addresses the technical and economic aspects of ferry service between Bar Harbor and Schoodic Peninsula (see chart, Figure 5-1). Candidate routes, terminals, and boats are identified and selected, and the economic model for ferry service exercised, with demand inputs as developed in Chapter 4. These analyses are for the seasonal and year round ferry services included in Transportation Alternatives 3 and 4, respectively.

5.1 Overview

5.1.1 Current conditions

Local passenger boat operations are and have been in recent years predominantly excursion services. Two whale watching companies, an "underwater" excursion, and another naturalist excursion operate from Bar Harbor. There is also a square rigged sailing vessel excursion operating twice daily from Bar Harbor. All of these services are seasonal.

Three ferry services currently operate from Mount Desert Island. Bay Ferries runs a 90 meter long high speed catamaran (Incat design and build, approximately 43 knots) from their terminal just north of downtown Bar Harbor to Yarmouth, Nova Scotia. Service is twice daily and is seasonal.

Bar Harbor Ferries has a new service running from the Harbor Point dock to the Winter Harbor Marina dock. The service caters to the recreational market in both directions, with 46' long wooden monohull (service speed of 8-9 knots). The run takes about 50 minutes. Commuter rates with early morning and evening runs were offered early in the 2001 season, but have been discontinued because of low ridership.

The Beal and Bunker Mail Boat Ferry runs from Northeast Harbor south to the Cranberry Isles, providing year round mail service and ferry service with a seasonally adjusted schedule (six trips daily in the summer, and three or four trips daily in the offseason). The boat is a 44' long monohull giving 20 minute service to Great Cranberry 30 minute service to Islesford.

The Maine State Ferry Service operates from Bass Harbor on southwest MDI to Swans Island year round, offering passenger and freight service, as well as providing gasoline delivery to the island. Service is five or six times daily in the summer and shoulder seasons, and four or five times daily in the offseason, depending on the day traveled.

5.1.2 Integration with other projects and studies

The only current or recently completed project or study which specifically addresses ferry service from Bar Harbor to Schoodic Peninsula was the Hancock County Planning Commission's (HCPC) "Schoodic Bar Harbor Ferry Feasibility Study", completed in 1998. It considered only commuter traffic and was based on a coordinated survey effort among workers at major employers on Mount Desert Island. Its finding was that a ferry from Schoodic could be compete with cars on a time basis, but that "only 27 persons" showed a "definite interest" in using it.

Public perception has been that the HCPC report returned a negative finding. A careful reading, however, reveals that potential undercounting of commuters into Bar Harbor and the prospect for growth on Schoodic plus reuse of the Navy base could translate into greater demand. The report alludes to tourist users without including them in demand projections and also refers to "inadequate" docking facilities in Schoodic. The dock infrastructure situation has changed (see below) and the demand from multiple markets is much better understood here as a result of the work presented in Chapters 4 and 5.

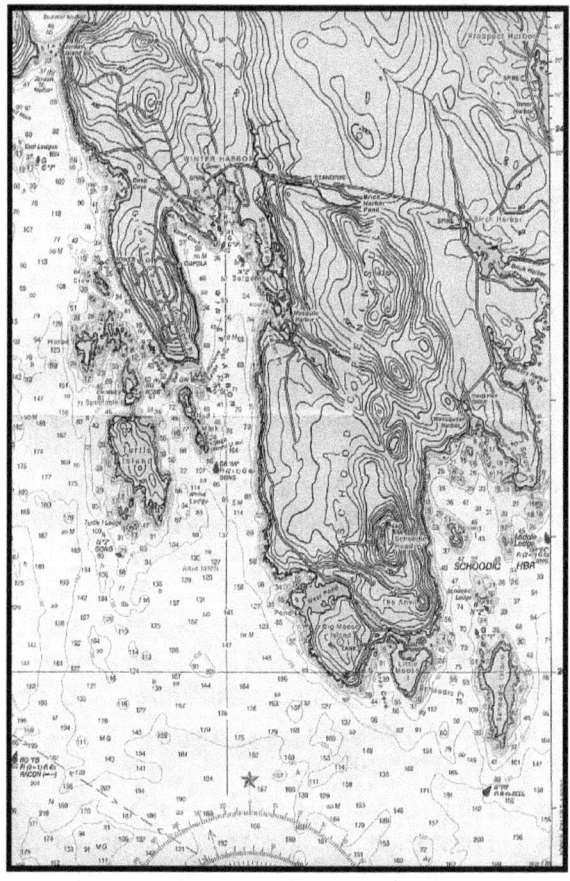

Source: NOAA Chart #13318

Figure 5-1
Schoodic Peninsula and Adjacent Waters

The Maine State DOT's Strategic Passenger Transportation Plan (Maine State DOT, 1999) calls for new regional links in all modes. Bangor is designated a "Gateway Intermodal Hub" and there is a concept plan to provide a rail link between the Bangor and Trenton-Bar Harbor Airports. Several new regional ferry service links are planned and Rockland terminal project is in the detail design stage. The Rockland terminal would provide new service to Portland and Bar Harbor; the Bay Ferries line has expressed interest in operating the service. The projected impact of this service on visitation to MDI is unknown and does not factor into these ferry demand calculations.

The prospect of travelers arriving in the Acadia area by this mode is, however, encouraging for the future of local ferry service.

5.2 Candidate Terminals

The inventory of candidate terminals for a future ferry service accounts for navigational approach conditions, depth and bottom characteristics, infrastructure (dock, float(s), parking, amenities), access from the roads network, and proximity to target markets. The selection of the best candidates is a qualitative judgment based on knowledge and experience of project staff.

The Schoodic Peninsula docks receive detailed consideration because there are significant operational and financial differences among them. It is taken here as a given that a ferry service will operate from Bar Harbor; therefore, the docks there do not receive the same scrutiny. Brief descriptions of the potentially available Bar Harbor docks follow the assessments of the Schoodic docks below.

5.2.1 Schoodic Peninsula

5.2.1.1 South Gouldsboro dock (private)

The South Gouldsboro dock is an inactive, privately owned structure co-located with an active commercial fishing dock and a large, tidally fed lobster pound. The dock is approximately 100' long and 35' wide (see Figure 5-2) and constructed of wooden pilings and planking; its condition is generally poor with much rot in the intertidal area and unsafe planking on the surface. A major reconstruction is needed and the owner states he plans to rebuild its base with granite ballast.

Figure 5-2
South Gouldsboro Dock

There is no cost estimate available for this work, but comparison to a similar project in Casco Bay, Maine is insightful. The Bustins Island Village Corporation, a political sub-entity of the Town of Freeport, has developed an estimate and the 2001 annual Corporation meeting authorized funding in the amount of $135,000 (Bustins Island

Village Corporation, 2001) to rebuild a wooden dock with granite pilings. The Bustins Island dock will be approximately 75' long and eight feet wide, only about 17% of the surface area of the South Gouldsboro dock (assuming that the future configuration would remain the same). The Bustins Island dock estimate could reasonably be multiplied by a factor of three or four; therefore, funding on the order $400,000 appears to be a reasonably conservative estimate for reconstruction of the South Gouldsboro dock, with floating crane and materials the major expenses.

The South Gouldsboro anchorage is afforded some protection by Stave and Jordan Islands to the west and south, but is not otherwise a well protected harbor. Boats at anchor are as close to shore as the limited minimum depth allows and there is currently no channel that would allow easy, direct passage of a relatively large passenger boat into the dock. Low tide depths to a muddy bottom, particularly on spring tides, would likely restrict or passage of boats with even four feet of draft. Furthermore, the available depth decreases closer to shore and probably rules out shortening the dock as a cost limiting measure for reconstruction. Some dredging would probably be necessary whatever the final configuration of the dock for reliable passenger ferry service. Finally, it has been reported that this area ices over in some winters (HCPC, 1998).

Access from USR 1 to the South Gouldsboro dock is good, only 3.4 miles on SR 186 and less than a quarter mile on Shore Road. Available parking at the dock is nonexistent at this time as the property lines to privately owned land press quite close to the dock head. The owner submits that lease or purchase of land about 1/10 mile up the road, currently used for storage of boats, cars, and other items, could serve the purpose. The likelihood of this outcome is not known and the needs of commuters for smooth intermodal transfer would not be served in any case.

Finally, it must be noted that other users of the South Gouldsboro anchorage and docks have expressed serious misgivings about a regularly scheduled ferry service there. Local user input is an important consideration in the project planning and implementation process.

5.2.1.2   Winter Harbor

Two dock sites in Winter Harbor offer a much better protected terminal than South Gouldsboro, although at a longer distance over more exposed waters from Bar Harbor. Grindstone Neck and Schoodic Peninsula bound the greater harbor on the west and east, respectively, and Turtle, Mark, and Ned Islands protect the southern entrance. Three separate inner anchorages (Sand Cove, Inner Winter Harbor, and Henry Cove) lie at its northern end (see chart, Figure 5-1 and aerial photograph, Figure 5-3).

Winter Harbor Town Dock

The Winter Harbor Town dock fronts on the west portion of the inner harbor, a very well protected anchorage, with intensive commercial and recreational use. It is well maintained and its construction is of both granite and wooden pilings (see Figure 5-4). The float is currently used by small tender boats on the shoreward side and by transient boats, mostly commercial fishermen, on the seaward side. The depth would be adequate for a commercial passenger boat. The approach through the anchorage does not afford a channel for ease of navigation by a relatively larger boat.

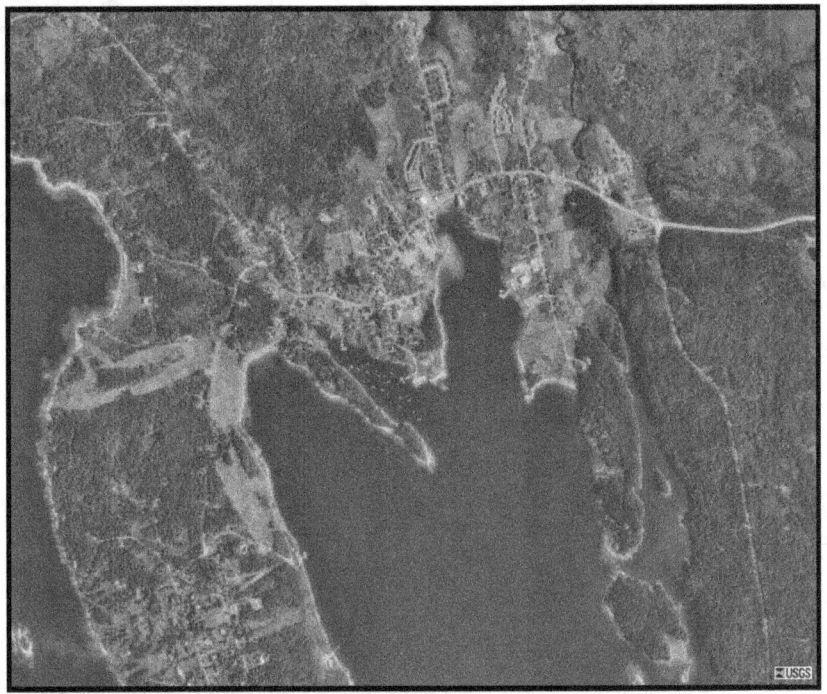

Source U.S. Geodetic Survey Website

Figure 5-3
Winter Harbor Aerial Photograph

Figure 5-4
Winter Harbor Town Dock

Access to the Winter Harbor Town dock is not direct, involving two local roads from SR 186 in the downtown, the second of which is a steep and winding track through a residential area to the head of the dock. There is limited reserved and open parking there and no area for expansion without the taking of adjacent land for the purpose. Current usage of the lot by commercial and recreational boaters would probably not allow for ferry parking. As in South Gouldsboro, the sentiment of local users seems to be rather strongly against this additional use of the dock.

Marina dock (private)

The Winter Harbor Marina dock is situated on the east side of the east part of the inner harbor. The location is also well protected; the approach, however, is much less congested than that of the Town dock or the South Gouldsboro dock. Depth is adequate at all tides (8' at low tide) for any of the boats under consideration and no winter icing conditions are reported.

The "hammerhead", L-shaped dock is in good condition, founded entirely on granite, and surfaced with a fine stone mixture. The float pictured (Figure 5-5) was on the landward side of the hammerhead at the time of the project team's last visit and was adequate for the tie-up of tenders and the occasional docking of Bar Harbor Ferry. The owner was in the process of expanding the floats to the seaward sides of the hammerhead in the summer of 2001 and also intends to move the tenders and all recreational activity to a separate dock just to the north (schedule for this change unknown).

Access to this dock is relatively straightforward, approximately ¼ mile on a local road from SR 186 in downtown Winter Harbor, and about 6.5 miles from USR 1 via SR 186. The marina's owner has already undertaken to provide extensive parking on-site (see Section 6.2).

5.2.1.3   Sorrento Town dock

The project team visited the Sorrento Town facility and found a well built dock and adequately sized float for the purpose of a passenger ferry in the required size range. However, access from USR 1 is poor, there is very little nearby parking, and the dock's location simply does not serve the Park Service's needs on Schoodic Peninsula. The Sorrento dock was dropped from further consideration.

5.2.1.4   Summary

The Winter Harbor Marina dock offers the best facility from the standpoints of navigation, condition of the dock infrastructure, ease of access and parking, and freedom from political friction. The dock is not the best in terms of access from USR 1 and maximizing commuter demand, but it clearly serves the Park Service's interests most effectively, as the facility closest to the Winter Harbor Park entrance and the most convenient location for possible future Schoodic Peninsula bus service links.

The other Schoodic Peninsula docks examined each had multiple and significant problems which would require one or more of the following: serious capital investment in infrastructure; navigational improvements; and a significant public education and publicity effort to garner the political good will of neighbors and co-users. It must be added that none of the Schoodic docks currently meet the access requirements of the

Americans with Disabilities Act (ADA). The stringent provisions of access at
Government facilities would not apply directly to the privately owned docks, but major
reconstruction would mean provision of at least "reasonable accommodations" under
the law. The 12::1 slope requirement (for the gangway) would likely be the most difficult
compliance item, given tidal heights of 12 feet and higher.

Figure 5-5
Winter Harbor Marina Dock

5.2.2 Bar Harbor

It is often said that Bar Harbor is not a harbor at all; its shoreline is exposed to both
north and south wind and waves except, in the former case, when the sand bar to Bar
Island (after which the town is named) emerges at low tide. The assumption for this
study is that one dock or another will emerge for use by a future ferry service; the
choice would cause negligible impact to ferry route times and schedules, but local bus
connections would require some adjustment for the particular location. All docks will
have issues of parking availability downtown and exposure to wind and waves at
various times.

From north to south, the docks and landmarks are: Bay Ferries Terminal, College of the
Atlantic docks, the tidal bar, the Bar Harbor Inn Pier, the 1 West Street docks
(whalewatcher and other excursions), the Harbor Place pier and Bar Harbor public
dock, and the Bar Harbor Inn Pier (see aerial photograph, Figure 5-6).

The 1 West Street dock is afforded the best protection from wind and waves of the
group with lees from Harbor Place dock to the south and a privately owned dock to the
north (see Figure 5-7). All the downtown docks face the Bar Harbor anchorage, which
is crowded and relatively close to shore during the summer. Any operational route
would have to include significant "go slow" time and an approach via the navigational
channel.

The Bar Harbor Inn Pier lies just south of the tidal bar granite construction, with hotel building covering the most of the dock's surface and several floats located around the perimeter for recreational use. The current use of the dock probably rules it out as a candidate for this service.

The Bar Harbor public dock is given over to use by fishing boats, recreational fishermen, and other boaters. Any commercial service use here would require public discourse and accommodation by the Town government. ADA access here is problematic for the same reasons given in the discussion of the Schoodic Peninsula docks.

Source: U.S. Geodetic Survey Website

Figure 5-6
Bar Harbor Aerial Photo

Figure 5-6
1 West Street Dock, Harbor Place Dock in Background

The College of the Atlantic and Bay Ferries docks lie north of the downtown and the "bar". Their potential for these purposes was not substantively explored, particularly not in terms of the organizations' willingness to consider such a service. These docks are at a greater distance from the downtown business area and the large businesses to which commuters would be traveling and, as at the downtown locations, parking availability is an issue.

5.3 Candidate Routes

Ferry service between Mount Desert Island and Schoodic Peninsula would traverse Frenchman Bay, a partially protected waterway of the Atlantic Ocean. The Bay spans between four and five nautical miles from its southern point (between Schooner Head on MDI and Big Moose Island) to its northern extreme between Cape Levi on MDI Waukeag Neck (Town of Sorrento); its length is approximately 8 nautical miles. Mount Desert Island lies to the west, Schoodic Peninsula to the east, and the mainland to the north, including the towns of Sullivan, Sorrento, and Ashville.

The two routes under consideration both originate in Bar Harbor, and would provide service to either South Gouldsboro or Winter Harbor. In each case, Frenchman Bay challenges mariners with long fetches for wind from varying directions, while numerous islands offer lee from both north and south winds.

Weather data indicate that Frenchman Bay receives relatively even amounts of precipitation on a month to month basis, (Acadia National Park, 1994), but the wind patterns vary seasonally. Wind intensity rises in the fall and winter and the direction tends to be from the north. Reports from local mariners indicate that storms in fall, winter, and spring can come from both the north and south and that occasional service cancellations would be likely. Spring and summer bring lighter winds, with frequent onshore southwest winds. The wind direction on a given day will influence the mariner's choice of exact route for the smoothest, fastest service.

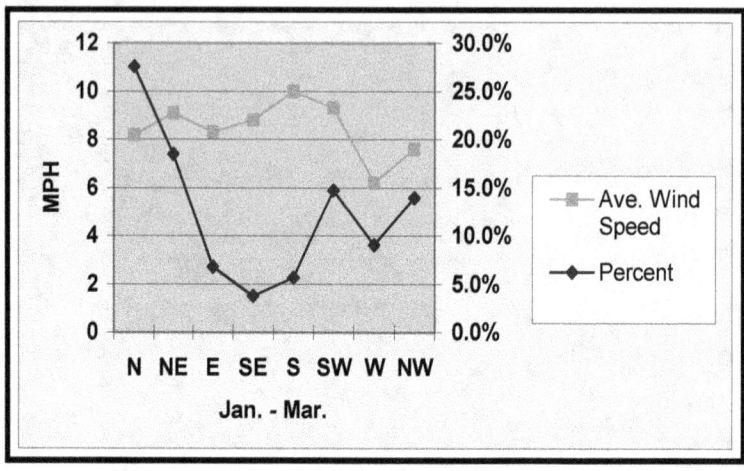

Source: National Weather Service, Portland, Maine

Figure 5-8
January – March Wind Data, 1998 - 2000

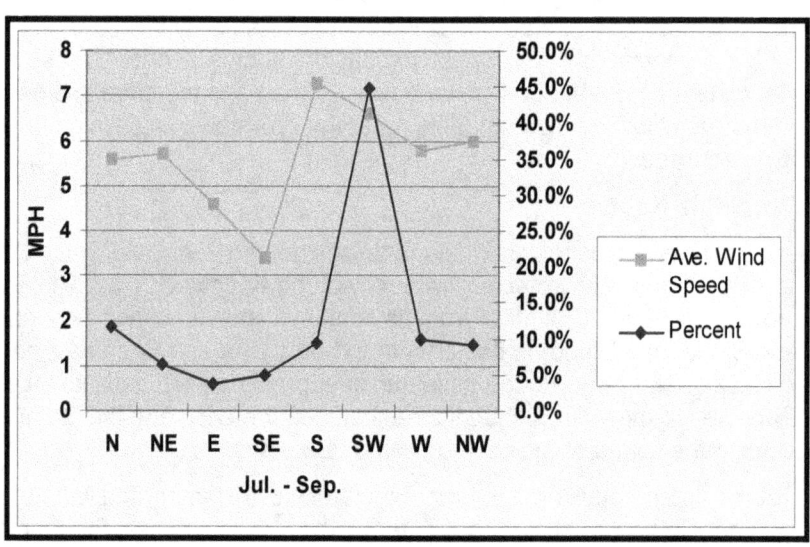

Source: National Weather Service, Portland, Maine

Figure 5-9
July – September Wind Data, 1998 - 2000

5.3.1 Bar Harbor to South Gouldsboro

The route between Bar Harbor and South Gouldsboro is approximately 4.69 nautical miles one way, and would be fairly direct. The Porcupine Islands lie in a line about ENE from Bar Harbor and extend about 2/3 of the distance across Frenchman Bay. The Islands would provide a lee from either northerly or southerly winds. In the latter case (common during the spring and summer months), the more protected route is to the north of the Porcupines and also would offer lee from Ironbound Island once to the east of Long Porcupine. Northerly winds, more prevalent in the winter, would dictate the more protected route south of the islands. In either case, the mariner departing Bar Harbor would run about ENE parallel to the Porcupine Islands and in their lee, make for Stave Island Harbor (between Stave and Jordan Islands), and turn north for the South Gouldsboro dock at Bunker Harbor.

The anchorage at Bunker Harbor is congested in the summer, with boats within 100' of the docks, riding in shallow water (occasionally grounding in some cases) at low tide. The approach would be slow for at least the last ¼ mile, and a passenger boat of the size considered herein would have to maneuver in tight quarters to approach the dock.

The route would be reversed for the run to Bar Harbor. The approach to the docks there would be at slow speed for the last ¼ to ½ mile, as the mariner would probably choose to approach via the channel at the south end of the anchorage (Bald Porcupine Island and the breakwater) and turn northwest along the Bar Harbor waterfront.

5.3.2 Bar Harbor to Winter Harbor

The Bar Harbor to Winter Harbor route would be an approximately 7.4 nautical mile run. The boat, on departing Bar Harbor, would follow the channel north of Bald Porcupine Island, turn approximately ESE and run south of Ironbound Island, and then turn east for the entrance to the marked channel along Grindstone Neck (Winter Harbor). Bad weather from the south might dictate running north of Ironbound Island and turning southeast through the channel at Halibut Hole; this course adds over a mile to the run and affords only limited relief from the weather.

The channel entrance is at the No. 5 green light north of Crow Island. The channel runs SSW about 1 nautical mile to the red-green light at Roaring Bull, then east between Grindstone Ledge and Ned Island to Winter Harbor. Finally, the course would be north about 1 ½ nautical miles to the Marina dock in Winter Harbor. The approach to the dock would be at service speed except for the last ¼ mile. There would also be some reduction in speed through the Grindstone Neck channel.

5.4 Passenger Boat Selection and Description

The identification of candidate boats for the route analysis followed upon conversations with local operators, application of common sense parameters as to service schedule, and review of the Volpe Center's U.S. ferry services data base. The desired attributes were:

- *Monohull and catamaran* – The logic is that planning for a modern ferry operation must consider both types.

- *Length* – The desired length is less than 65', because of the regulatory breakpoint in the Coast Guard regulations for Subchapter "T" boats affecting several construction and operational (and, therefore, cost) areas, and the sense that nothing larger is appropriate for the service, both in terms of aesthetics and the likely demand for ferry service.

- *Service speed* – The experience of a current operator with a slow boat and the basic demand versus time relationship (especially for commuter service) dictate more speed than currently available services offer. A minimum of 18 knots for a well designed monohull or a small catamaran is reasonable.

- *Capacity* – Passenger capacity of between 50 and 100. This is below the Coast Guard Subchapter T breakpoint of 149, would certainly suffice for either year round or seasonal commuter service, and is manageably sized for tourist and recreational service. In the latter instance, it fits the possibility of a ranger onboard for Park visitor education (as the Bar Harbor Ferry currently offers) and the lower passenger loads that may be expected in shoulder seasons.

- *Age* – A used vessel was decided upon in order to limit the purchase price and annual debt service. The boat should have built within the last five to ten years, young in terms of passenger service and offering a somewhat reduced purchase price.

Project staff reviewed industry journals and the Volpe Center Ferry Lines Data Base and identified several candidate monohulls and catamarans. These were proven vessels, in service elsewhere. Final selections were on the basis of the best fit to the specifications shown previously. The identities of the boats, builders, and current operators are not included here.

HULL TYPE	MONOHULL	CATAMARAN
Length (ft)	50'	78'
Breadth (ft)	13.7'	26.2'
Depth(ft)	7.1'	8.5'*
Draft (ft)	4.5'*	4.9'
Passengers	64	100
Service Speed	22 knots	27 knots
Engine Type	2 Diesel	2 MTU
Power	1420 hp	2100 hp
Fuel Consumption at Service Speed	60 gal/hr	100 gal/hr
Age (as of 2001)	4 years	3 years
Approx. Price (2001)*	$500,000	$1,200,000

* Estimated value.

Table 5-1
Particulars of Selected Boats

5.4.1 Monohull

The 50' monohull chosen offers the speed required for reasonably short commuter service head time (frequency of round trip service, including loading and unloading) and one way trip duration. The boat can travel at lower speed if so desired, e.g., for the purposes of tourist service. The draft allows for passage into most area harbors at low tide. Passenger capacity should suffice for all but the busiest peak tourist demands. Both the monohull and the catamaran selected are relatively young (as of 2001); however, they would be eight and seven years old, respectively, at the projected start of service in 2005. The capital purchase cost for each will therefore have decreased significantly by that time.

5.4.2 Catamaran

The catamaran is typical of the type built in United States shipyards in the early stage of the industry's move into the production of high speed vessels. Licensing agreements between the Australian designers and shipbuilders and U.S. firms (e.g., Nichols Brothers and Gladding-Hearn) spawned production first of these smaller sized (length = 50' – 100') catamarans and has progressed to larger sized boats (length = 120' – 180') in recent years. The market has remained strong for the smaller boats and the number of domestic shipyards capable of their construction has increased steadily. A new or used boat of the type described should be readily available at reasonable terms at the projected date of service startup.

The draft and passenger capacity of the selected catamaran are suitable for the selected harbors, although there will probably be more excess capacity for many trips than for the monohull. The speed of this boat affords even lower head times and trip times than the monohull, although at the price of greater fuel consumption. Debt service and maintenance costs will also be higher for this boat.

5.5 Service and Economic Parameters

The notional services described herein would each draw patronage from at least three target markets: commuters and reverse commuters between the Schoodic – "Down East" area, vocational and educational users of the future facility at the Schoodic Navy base, and recreational users traveling in either direction. The analyses of seasonal and year round services each include twelve scenarios, inputs for which are the following:

- **Boats** –Service by either one or two monohulls, or one catamaran. Trip times and head times vary for each.
- **Demand** – Both high and low demand inputs based upon the stipulated base reuse concepts.
- **Year** – Both the initial (2005) and end (2015) years of the look period.

Economic and operational factors common to all scenarios appear in Table 5-2.

There several points for the reader to bear in mind:

- The value of the owner's initial equity is not included in the model.
- The assumed fares for these services were derived through industry comparisons and discussions with local transportation providers. There was, in particular, the realization that commuter fares must not exceed the perceived trip-to-work expenses for Schoodic commuters, i.e., gasoline costs.
- The term of loan spans the full look period for the analysis and debt service is therefore the same in each case for 2005 and 2015.

- Maintenance costs rise as the vessels age and are therefore higher in 2015. Marine hull insurance costs likewise decline with age.
- Insurance and administrative costs tied to passenger units vary depending on reuse scenario and year.
- Fares are assumed constant in 2001 dollars throughout, although they would be likely to rise in real terms.

Factor	Value
Annual capital depreciation of vessel	2.3%
Initial owner's equity	20%
Interest rate	10%
Term of loan	15 years (equal payment schedule)
Annual maintenance cost	3.5%: 60% fixed costs; 40% tied to operating hours, absolute cost rises with actual hours
Crew	(1) master; (1) mate
Fuel	$1.41/gallon
Lubricant	0.4% of fuel consumption, $8.00/gallon
Docking fees	$0.10/passenger, each terminal
Marine hull insurance	2.0% of vessel value
Protection and indemnity insurance	$0.35/passenger
Marketing, advertising, sales	3.5% of total revenues
General administration	$5,000/year + $0.50/passenger
Fare – commuter	$3.00 each way
Fare – recreational	$20.00/$12.00 round trip adult/child

Table 5-2
Ferry Economic and Operational Factors

The schedules are based upon the times and distances appearing in Table 5-3 for both the monohull and catamaran. Service are shown slightly reduced from the rated values to account for the effects of wind and waves, as well as the slight losses in speed expected as a boat ages.

Bar Harbor to Winter Harbor, monohull			
	Speed (knots)	Distance (nm)	Time (min)
Slow speed out	10	0.50	3.00
Service speed	20	6.38	19.14
Slow speed in	10	0.50	3.00
Totals/averages	17.61	7.38	25.14

Bar Harbor to Winter Harbor, catamaran			
	Speed (knots)	Distance (nm)	Time (min)
Slow speed out	10	0.50	3.00
Service speed	25	6.38	15.31
Slow speed in	10	0.50	3.00
Totals/averages	20.78	7.38	21.31

Table 5-3
Ferry Run Times

5.5.1 Seasonal service (commuter & recreational)

Seasonal service is for an assumed 26-week period annually, including the summer and "shoulder" seasons which altogether are the months of May through October. All cost and revenue factors are tied directly to the actual service modeled, i.e., one way trips and operating hours for those months. Annual debt service and marine hull insurance costs are reduced to an estimated 60% of the calculated total on the assumption that the boat(s) would enter winter service somewhere else and that layup time would be shared between the two seasonal services.

Both commuter service schedule, during weekday morning and evening peak hours, and scheduled recreational runs seven days per week would be constant during the six month service period. Frequencies and schedules vary according to the boat(s) in each scenario. The schedule for the single monohull appears in Table 5-4 (others are in Appendix F) and the daily service and run time summary in Table 5-5. Schedule cells shaded in yellow indicate the start of service in the morning and departure times with longer than minimum layover times, usually between commuter and recreational runs.

Schedule I - summer - weekdays				Schedule II - summer - weekends			
Winter Harbor	Bar Harbor	Bar Harbor	Winter Harbor	Winter Harbor	Bar Harbor	Bar Harbor	Winter Harbor
Leave	Arrive	Leave	Arrive	Leave	Arrive	Leave	Arrive
Morning				Morning			
5:15 AM	5:40 AM	5:55 AM	6:20 AM	8:00 AM	8:25 AM	8:40 AM	9:05 AM
6:35 AM	7:00 AM	7:15 AM	7:40 AM	9:20 AM	9:45 AM	10:00 AM	10:25 AM
7:55 AM	8:20 AM	9:00 AM	9:25 AM	10:40 AM	11:05 AM	11:20 AM	11:45 AM
10:00 AM	10:25 AM	11:00 AM	11:25 AM	11:45 AM	12:10 PM	12:25 PM	12:51 PM
Afternoon				Afternoon			
12:00 PM	12:25 PM	1:00 PM	1:25 PM	1:06 PM	1:31 PM	1:46 PM	2:11 PM
2:00 PM	2:25 PM	3:30 PM	3:55 PM	2:26 PM	2:51 PM	3:06 PM	3:31 PM
4:10 PM	4:35 PM	4:50 PM	5:15 PM	3:46 PM	4:11 PM	4:26 PM	4:51 PM
5:30 PM	5:55 PM	6:10 PM	6:35 PM	5:06 PM	5:32 PM	5:47 PM	6:12 PM
6:50 PM	7:15 PM	7:30 PM	7:55 PM	6:27 PM	6:52 PM	7:07 PM	7:32 PM

**Table 5-4
Summer Ferry Schedule, (1) Monohull**

Summary: Winter Harbor, Summer Service							
		Weekday			Weekend		
		freq.	run time(hrs)	layover (hrs)	freq.	run time(hrs)	layover (hrs)
78' Cat.	commuter	10	3.55	2.50	7	2.49	1.75
	recreational	10	3.55	2.50	13	4.62	3.25
	total	20	7.10	5.00	20	7.10	5.00
50' Mono hull	commuter	9	3.77	2.25	7	2.93	1.75
	recreational	9	3.77	2.25	11	4.61	2.75
	total	18	7.54	4.50	18	7.54	4.50
(2) 50' Monohulls	commuter	20	9.09	5.00	8	3.64	2.00
	recreational	18	8.18	4.50	16	7.27	4.00
	total	38	17.27	9.50	24	10.91	6.00

Table 5-5
Daily Summer Service Run Time Summary

5.5.2 Year round service (commuter & recreational)

Year round service would run for 50 weeks annually, allowing two weeks for layup, maintenance, and repair during the winter and providing for the needs of commuters and Navy base users during all seasons. Schedules are similar to those for the six month seasonal service during peak and shoulder seasons. Commuter service runs are maintained in the off season. Weekday recreational runs are reduced to four daily and weekend runs total ten per day. The single monohull schedule appears in Table 5-6 and others are in Appendix F. The daily run time summary for winter service appears in Table 5-7.

Schedule III - winter - weekdays				Schedule IV - winter - weekends			
Winter Harbor Leave	Bar Harbor Arrive	Bar Harbor Leave	Winter Harbor Arrive	Winter Harbor Leave	Bar Harbor Arrive	Bar Harbor Leave	Winter Harbor Arrive
Morning				Morning			
5:15 AM	5:40 AM	5:55 AM	6:20 AM	8:00 AM	8:25 AM	8:40 AM	9:05 AM
6:35 AM	7:00 AM	7:15 AM	7:40 AM	10:00 AM	10:25 AM	10:40 AM	11:05 AM
7:55 AM	8:20 AM	10:00 AM	10:25 AM	11:20 AM	11:45 AM	12:00 PM	12:25 PM
11:30 AM	11:55 AM						
Afternoon				Afternoon			
		1:00 PM	1:25 PM	1:00 PM	1:25 PM	1:40 PM	2:05 PM
2:30 PM	2:55 PM	3:30 PM	3:55 PM	3:00 PM	3:25 PM	3:40 PM	4:05 PM
4:10 PM	4:35 PM	4:50 PM	5:15 PM				
5:30 PM	5:55 PM	6:10 PM	6:35 PM				
6:50 PM	7:15 PM	7:30 PM	7:55 PM				

Table 5-6
Winter Ferry Schedule, (1) Monohull

Summary: Winter Harbor, Winter Service							
		Weekday			Weekend		
		freq.	run time(hrs)	layover (hrs)	freq.	run time(hrs)	layover (hrs)
78' Cat.	commute	10	3.55	2.50	4	1.42	1.00
	recreational	6	2.13	1.50	6	2.13	1.50
	total	16	5.68	4.00	10	3.55	2.50
50' Mono hull	comm.	9	3.77	2.25	4	1.68	1.00
	rec.	7	2.93	1.75	6	2.51	1.50
	total	16	6.70	4.00	10	4.19	2.50
(2) 50' Monohulls	comm.	20	9.09	5.00	6	2.73	1.50
	rec.	8	3.64	2.00	6	2.73	1.50
	total	28	12.72	7.00	12	5.45	3.00

Table 5-7
Daily Winter Service Run Time Summary

5.6 Demand

The demand calculations for all three ferry service scenarios are based on voyage time, headway times, and distances to commuter residences, derived separately for commuter and recreational trips. National and Park-specific survey data provide mode preference percentages which are applied to the demographic, land use, and visitation data for the ferry usage results, context of the Transportation Alternatives, Reuse Concepts 1 and 3 (high and low use intensity), and in the years 2005 and 2015. Tables 5-8, 5-9, and 5-10 present the daily demand results for all scenarios involving the single monohull service (full data set appears in Appendix F).

5.6.1 Commuters

The majority of the commuters would originate east of Gouldsboro and drive personal vehicles to Winter Harbor via Rte 186. The commuter fare structure has been deliberately kept low, so as to be affordable for most residents. The weekly cost of the $6 per day round trip would be roughly equivalent to what many are paying for gasoline for their automobile commutes. It is possible that a commuter subsidy would enable the operator to charge this fare value; none is included in the economic assessment, however.

The two monohull ferry service would capture the greatest number of commuter trips due to its frequency of service. The single catamaran service was very close to the two monohull option in all scenarios due to its short run time, while the single monohull service was a close third. The ranges in annual seasonal ridership numbers in the "Low 2005" scenario were small among the three ferry services, ranging from a low of 3,770 for the single monohull, to a high of 4,290 for the two monohull option. In the "High 2015" scenario, the single monohull service would attract a low of 5,460 commuters while the two monohull service would draw 6,370 commuters. The year round commuter trips followed the same trends. Total ridership would be higher in all cases than for seasonal service, as one would expect, but there would be declines in average daily use.

Table 5-11 shows the results for patronage of the one monohull service for all seasonal and year round scenarios (full set of results appears in Appendix F), resulting from extrapolation of the daily numbers. Annual commuter patronage appears in the $6 fare columns.

Year		Commuter		Recreational		Total
	Concept	Bar Harbor Bound	Schoodic Bound	Bar Harbor Bound	Schoodic Bound	Average Daily Roundtrips
2005						
	High-Concept 3	24	9	46	171	250
	Low-Concept 1	24	5	20	110	159
2015						
	High-Concept 3	32	10	63	193	298
	Low-Concept 1	29	8	28	131	196

Table 5-8
Average Daily Roundtrips, 1 Monohull, Seasonal

Year		Commuter		Recreational		Total
	Concept	Bar Harbor Bound	Schoodic Bound	Bar Harbor Bound	Schoodic Bound	Average Daily Roundtrips
2005						
	High-Concept 3	18	3	18	12	51
	Low-Concept 1	18	2	18	8	46
2015						
	High-Concept 3	24	3	24	14	65
	Low-Concept 1	22	2	22	9	55

Table 5-9
Average Daily Roundtrips, 1 Monohull, Off-Season

Year		Commuter		Recreational		Total
	Concept	Bar Harbor Bound	Schoodic Bound	Bar Harbor Bound	Schoodic Bound	Average Daily Roundtrips
2005						
	High-Concept 3	21	6	32	92	151
	Low-Concept 1	21	4	19	59	103
2015						
	High-Concept 3	28	7	44	104	182
	Low-Concept 1	26	5	25	70	126

Table 5-10
Average Daily Roundtrips, 1 Monohull, Yearly

	Number of Round Trips, Annual							
	Seasonal Service				Year Round Service			
Fare	$6	$12	$20	Total	$6	$12	$20	Total
Year 2005								
Reuse Concept 1	**3,770**	**3,076**	**20,584**	**27,430**	**6,312**	**3,230**	**21,613**	**31,155**
Commuter Trips	3,770	0	0	3,770	6,312	0	0	6,312
Recreational Trips	0	3,076	20,584	23,660	0	3,230	21,613	24,843
Reuse Concept 3	**4,290**	**5,134**	**34,360**	**43,784**	**6,993**	**5,391**	**36,078**	**48,462**
Commuter Trips	4,290	0	0	4,290	6,993	0	0	6,993
Recreational Trips	0	5,134	34,360	39,494	0	5,391	36,078	41,469
Year 2015								
Reuse Concept 1	**4,810**	**3,762**	**25,176**	**33,748**	**7,960**	**3,950**	**26,435**	**38,345**
Commuter Trips	4,810	0	0	4,810	7,960	0	0	7,960
Recreational Trips	0	3,762	25,176	28,938	0	3,950	26,435	30,385
Reuse Concept 3	**5,460**	**6,057**	**40,535**	**52,052**	**8,983**	**6,360**	**42,561**	**57,904**
Commuter Trips	5,460	0	0	5,460	8,983	0	0	8,983
Recreational Trips	0	6,057	40,535	46,592	0	6,360	42,561	48,921

Note: Commuter fare = $6; recreational fares = $20 and $12, for adults and children.

Table 5-11
One Monohull Ferry Service: Patronage for All Scenarios

5.6.2 Recreational

Recreational trips would, in spite of a much higher fare structure relative to commuters, account for a tremendous majority of passengers and revenue for all scenarios. Examination of currently excursion fares in Bar Harbor, plus the desire to keep the model's assumptions conservative. The fare values used are roundtrips of $20 and $12 for adults and children (10 years and younger), respectively, somewhat lower than fares currently charged for similar services. It was assumed that children make up 13% of the total visitors (Ref Littlejohn).

The following examples illustrate the dominance of the recreational market. In the "Low 2005" seasonal use scenario for one monohull, the 23,660 recreational roundtrips account for 86% of total trips. In the "High 2015" seasonal use scenario for two monohulls, the 55,874 projected recreational roundtrips would be 90% of the total. As for commuter trips, recreational demand would be highest for the two monohull service, followed closely by the catamaran and single monohull services, in every case and for the same reasons of voyage time and head time. Year round use is only 10 to 20% more than the seasonal use due to the fact that recreational trips drop off significantly during the winter months.

Table 5-11 shows the results for patronage of the one monohull service for all seasonal and year round scenarios (full set of results appears in Appendix F).

5.7 Ferry Economic Model Results

The ferry economic model calculates costs of operation in detail, as described in Chapter 3. One example each of the detailed cost results appears in the subsections on both seasonal and year round services, for both 2005 and 2015 and the high and low revenue projections. Revenue inputs are per the demand calculations appearing previously, and appear here in both commuter and recreational categories. Summaries for all scenarios include total direct and indirect costs, as well as patronage data (passengers and revenue). Detailed cost and revenue results for all boats and scenarios appear in Appendix F.

5.7.1 Seasonal service

Seasonal service operation has the obvious effect of maximizing recreational revenues and minimizing operational costs such as labor and fuel. Table 5-12 is an example (one 50' monohull) of the detailed cost and aggregate revenue results (others appear in Appendix F). It shows that debt service and direct operating costs for the service are the same (in constant 2001 dollars) for both years 2005 and 2015 and the high and low reuse options. Indirect costs which correlate to patronage and gross revenues vary as expected, the latter due to demand variations explained in section 5.6.

The cost and patronage summary for all seasonal services and scenarios appears in Table 5-13. All scenarios show the potential for profitable operation, particularly the high end reuse options. Recreational patronage and fares are clearly the dominant elements of the potential success of seasonal service. This aspect is treated in more detail in subsection 5.7.3.

50' Monohull, Seasonal Operation	2005 High	2005 Low	2015 High	2015 Low
Vessel Debt Service	$ 37,757	$ 37,757	$ 37,757	$ 37,757
Direct Operating Costs				
Salaries, Wages and Benefits	$ 80,113	$ 80,113	$ 80,113	$ 80,113
Vessel Fuel and Lubricants	$ 89,885	$ 89,885	$ 89,885	$ 89,885
Vessel Maintenance Costs	$ 21,039	$ 21,039	$ 24,667	$ 24,667
Marine Hull Insurance	$ 5,973	$ 5,973	$ 4,758	$ 4,758
Direct Operating Costs Subtotal	$ 197,010	$ 197,010	$ 199,422	$ 199,422
Indirect Operating Costs				
Marketing and Advertising	$ 15,491	$ 9,424	$ 18,539	$ 11,550
Reservations & Sales	$ 11,618	$ 7,068	$ 13,904	$ 8,663
Docking Fees / Passenger Facility Charges / Shore Operations	$ 8,757	$ 5,486	$ 10,590	$ 6,750
Protection and Indemnity (P&I) Insurance	$ 30,649	$ 19,201	$ 37,066	$ 23,624
General Administration	$ 48,784	$ 32,430	$ 57,952	$ 38,748
Indirect Operating Costs Subtotal	$ 115,299	$ 73,609	$ 138,052	$ 89,335
Revenue- passenger fares	$774,548	$471,212	$926,944	$577,524
Net Annual Cash Flow Before Taxes	**$424,482**	**$162,836**	**$551,713**	**$251,010**

Table 5-12
Seasonal Service Finances, 50' Monohull

	50' Monohull		(2) X 50' Monohull		78' Catamaran	
	2005 High	**2005 Low**	**2005 High**	**2005 Low**	**2005 High**	**2005 Low**
Total Costs	$350,066	$308,376	$547,428	$498,046	$506,295	$457,251
Direct Costs + Debt Service	$234,767	$234,767	$411,162	$411,162	$373,679	$373,679
Indirect Costs	$115,299	$73,609	$136,266	$86,884	$132,616	$83,572
Patronage						
Commuter 2-way Fares	4,290	3,770	4,940	4,290	5,200	4,290
Commuter Revenue	$25,740	$22,620	$29,640	$25,740	$31,200	$25,740
Recreational 2-way Fares	39,494	23,660	47,138	28,410	45,500	27,118
Recreational Revenue	$748,808	$448,592	$893,736	$538,656	$862,680	$514,160
NET INCOME	**$424,482**	**$162,836**	**$375,948**	**$66,350**	**$387,585**	**$82,649**
	2015 High	**2015 Low**	**2015 High**	**2015 Low**	**2015 High**	**2015 Low**
Total Costs	$375,231	$326,514	$577,085	$520,576	$537,101	$482,650
Direct Costs + Debt Service	$237,180	$237,180	$415,406	$415,406	$381,021	$381,021
Indirect Costs	$138,052	$89,335	$161,679	$105,170	$156,080	$101,630
Patronage						
Commuter 2-way Fares	5,460	4,810	6,370	5,460	6,370	5,330
Commuter Revenue	$32,760	$28,860	$38,220	$32,760	$38,220	$31,980
Recreational 2-way Fares	47,492	28,938	55,874	34,580	53,690	33,306
Recreational Revenue	$894,184	$548,664	$1,059,368	$655,640	$1,017,960	$631,480
NET INCOME	**$551,713**	**$251,010**	**$520,503**	**$167,824**	**$519,079**	**$180,810**

Table 5-13
Seasonal Cost and Patronage Summary

5.7.2 Year round

Year round service presents a markedly different cost picture due to the fuel and labor costs associated with the extra hours of vessel operation, as well as the allocation of 100% of debt service costs to the budget. Revenues overall meanwhile rise only slightly since recreational use in the off-season is limited; commuter revenues rise proportionally with the extra operating time (for year round commuters only), but these represent a small fraction of total revenues. Only the single 50' monohull operation shows the potential for profit in all year round scenarios. The low end Navy base reuse alternative would result in net losses for both the catamaran and two monohull services in the years 2005 and 2015. Results are summarized in Table 5-14.

The operator of a year round service will face the added issues of winter weather and the possibilities of service cancellations and increased voyage times. The exposure of the Winter Harbor route means that both northeast storms and high winds from other quadrants will affect the captain's decisions as to route and speed. Voyage times are short enough to avoid the acute effects of motion sickness for most passengers, but higher frequency of passenger discomfort can be expected. Service cancellations and scheduled off-season maintenance layups will mean that the operator will have to substitute bus service for the ferry.

	50' Monohull		(2) X 50' Monohull		78' Catamaran	
	2005 High	2005 Low	2005 High	2005 Low	2005 High	2005 Low
Total Costs	$522,648	$478,591	$835,962	$783,747	$762,913	$710,917
Direct Costs + Debt Service	$396,584	$396,584	$687,038	$687,038	$617,681	$617,681
Indirect Costs	$126,064	$82,007	$148,924	$96,709	$145,232	$93,235
Patronage						
Commuter 2-way Fares	6,993	6,313	8,075	7,223	8,415	7,223
Commuter Revenue	$41,955	$37,875	$48,450	$43,335	$50,490	$43,335
Recreational 2-way Fares	41,469	24,843	49,495	29,829	47,775	28,474
Recreational Revenue	$786,252	$471,020	$938,428	$565,556	$905,812	$539,864
NET INCOME	$305,559	$30,304	$150,916	-$174,856	$193,389	-$127,718

	2015 High	2015 Low	2015 High	2015 Low	2015 High	2015 Low
Total Costs	$548,833	$499,199	$869,422	$808,985	$798,397	$740,046
Direct Costs + Debt Service	$399,509	$399,509	$691,829	$691,829	$626,800	$626,800
Indirect Costs	$149,325	$99,691	$177,593	$117,156	$171,596	$113,246
Patronage						
Commuter 2-way Fares	8,963	7,960	10,518	9,040	10,463	8,813
Commuter Revenue	$53,775	$47,760	$63,105	$54,240	$62,775	$52,875
Recreational 2-way Fares	48,921	30,385	58,668	36,309	56,374	34,971
Recreational Revenue	$927,540	$576,100	$1,112,344	$688,420	$1,068,848	$663,052
NET INCOME	$432,482	$124,661	$306,027	-$66,325	$333,226	-$24,119

Table 5-14
Year Round Cost and Patronage Summary

5.7.3 Summary

The economics model projects costs and revenues based on a set of specific assumptions previously described. The cost figures are conservatively high in some instances, particularly for fuel ($1.41/gallon is higher than many operators pay, at least in 2001) and the capital costs of the boats. Demand projections are also subject to some uncertainty and the actual numbers could be higher or lower than the analysis predicts; the fare bases, however, are conservatively low. The outlook for some form of ferry service is positive, even given the uncertainties. The opportunities in both commuter and recreational markets are tangible (especially given the conservative assumptions built into the model) and will brighten further as both Park visitation and area populations grow.

Figure 5-6 indicates that all seasonal service scenarios considered would be profitable. Year round service results in lower profits and, in the cases of catamaran and two monohull services, losses in the "low" reuse scenarios. It is important to point out the extent to which recreational revenues drive these results. Figure 5-7 presents those data graphically and shows that recreational revenues would be the lion's share in every case (92%-93% in "low reuse" scenarios, 94% - 95% in "high reuse" scenarios).

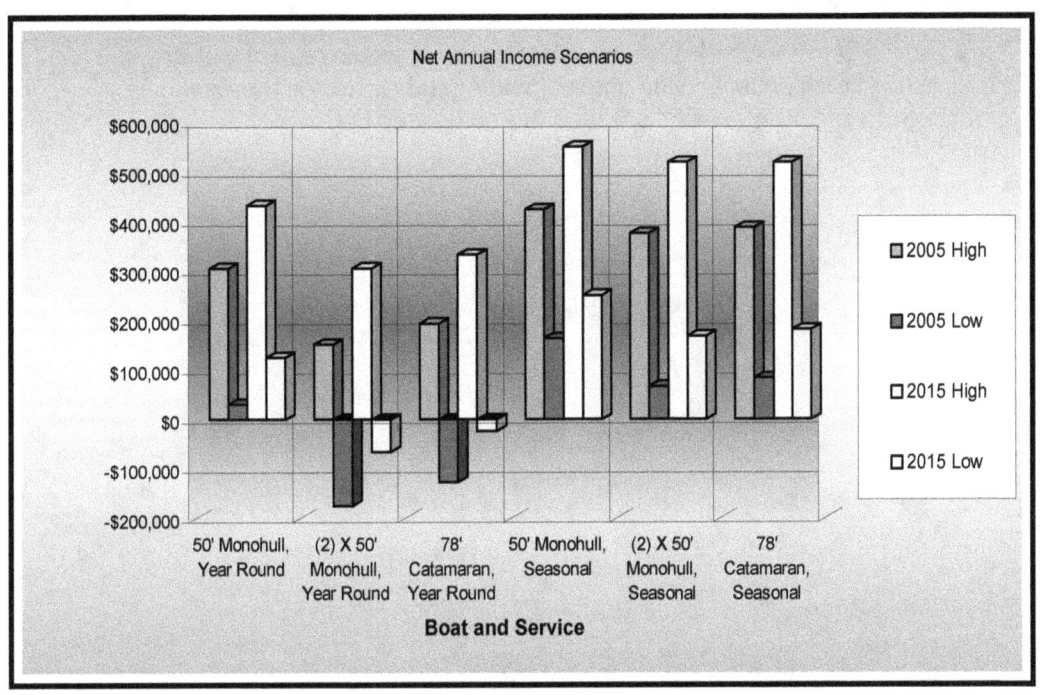

Figure 5-10
Net Income Summary for All Services

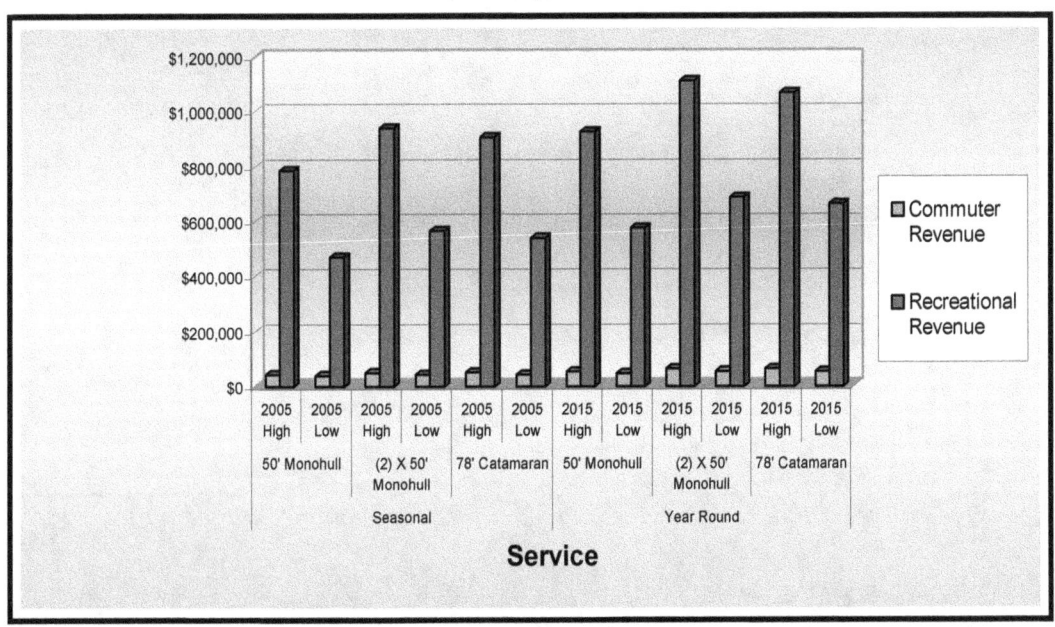

Figure 5-11
Revenue by Source for All Services

5.8 Bus Service Links

Ferry service between Bar Harbor and Winter Harbor would require well designed transit links at both ends, serving both commuter and recreational passengers, in order to succeed to its fullest extent. Specifics are addressed in Chapter 7.

6   Schoodic Bicycling Enhancement Options

A discussion of current conditions for bicycling in Schoodic Peninsula, currently applicable standards for bicycle paths, and the projected demand for future bicycling lead to a qualitative assessment of roadway improvements for the provision of bicycle paths and park-and-ride facilities. These improvements are not specifically linked to the Schoodic Transportation Alternatives advanced herein, but would support all of the "active" Alternatives, i.e., 2, 3, and 4.

6.1 Access and Use

The Schoodic Peninsula provides the bicyclist many opportunities to see picturesque views of the Maine seashore, woods, and coastal villages. This opportunity depends on the visitor's ability to bring a bicycle to the location and then to safely traverse the roadways and trails. Chapter 6 examines the bicyclist's options for transport to the area, the current state of bicycling opportunities, and options for the development or improvement of bicycle paths. A brief on the roadway and bicycle path standards prepared by the American Association of State Highways and Transportation Organizations (AASHTO) is included to highlight the identification of roadway deficiencies and suggested improvements.

6.1.1 Current conditions and goals

The bicyclist touring Schoodic Peninsula currently can use a 13.0 mile loop made up of six segments (identified in Table 6-1). All of the roads outside of the park (5.2 miles in total length) are two-way for both cars and bicycles. The road inside the park, with the exception of the road to Schoodic Point, is one-way (7.8 miles in total length) and dictates the direction of the bicyclist. The loop is paved surface throughout. The Park does not allow the use of bicycles on trails in the Schoodic parkland.

The roadway classification is based on design criteria and usage. Table 6-1 summarizes the roadway conditions observed and descriptive data collected, including lane configuration, volume of traffic, shoulders, speed, terrain, and striping for bicycling. The SR 186 segment has the highest volume in the loop with an average of 2,000 vehicles daily traveling this route. The volumes on all of the roadways peak during the summer time and drop off during the winter months.

No provision has been made on these roads to provide designated, safe bicycle paths. Bicyclists must avoid conflicts with vehicular traffic by using the shoulders, i.e., the portions of the roadways to the immediate right of the travel lane. The configuration of the shoulder and its composition are important considerations in the analysis of bicycle lanes. The roads of interest outside the park all have shoulders between two and four feet in width, made up of mostly of gravel and, occasionally, loose pavement.

The shoulders on the Park roads average less than one foot in width and are composed of dirt or grass. Coping stones were originally placed along the shoulder to limit vehicular traffic and they sometimes preclude use of the shoulder. There are several naturally occurring rock outcroppings along the roadway that limit or prevent use of the shoulder.

Current Conditions	Moore Road	Moore Rd inside of Park	Schoodic Point Road	Wonsqueak Rd inside of Park	E. Schoodic Road	SR 186
Description	Between Winter Harbor, SR 186 & Park Entrance, Frazer Point	Between Winter Harbor, Moore Rd & Road to Schoodic Point	Between Park Loop Road & Schoodic Point	Between Road to Schoodic Point and E. Schoodic Road	Between Birch Harbor, SR 186 & Park Entrance	Between Winter Harbor, Moore Rd & Birch Harbor, East Schoodic Rd
Lanes	1 lane each way	2 lanes one-way	1 lane each way	2 Lanes one-way	1 lane each way	1 lane each way
Length	1.25 miles	3.3 miles	1 miles	2.5 miles	1.8 miles	1.7 miles
Classification	Minor Collector	Minor Collector	Local Road	Minor Collector	Minor Collector	Major Collector
Yr 2000 Average Daily Traffic	800	700	700	700	1000	2000
Shoulder	2' - Gravel	1' - Dirt	None	1' - Dirt	2' - Gravel	3' - Gravel
Avg. Speed	35 mph	30 mph	25 mph	30 mph	35 mph	40 mph
Terrain	Gently Rolling	Level	Level	Level	Level	Gently Rolling
Accidents	Minor	Minor	Minor	Minor	Minor	Minor
Striping for bicycles	None	None	None	None	None	None
Bicycle Signage	None	None	None	None	None	None
Intersection Points	Some	None	One	None	Some	Some

Table 6-1
Current Conditions of Roadway for Bicyclists

Moore Road and East Schoodic Road are the Schoodic parkland entry and exit roads leading from and to SR 186, respectively, and they have an average speed of 35 mph. SR 186 was designed for more traffic at the higher speed of 40 mph. The Park road is 30 mph with some stretches that go down to 25 mph. The terrain is generally level with some sections with gently rolling hills. There have been, generally, few accidents, with no evidence seen of concentration in any particular locations. Accidents on the Park road, reported anecdotally to the project team, were mostly due to Navy personnel, especially during the winter months.

None of the roadways have lane striping or signage for bicyclists. This area is sparsely settled and has large tracts of undeveloped land; there are, therefore, very few access points onto the roadways.

6.1.2 AASHTO guidelines

Established in 1914, AASHTO has been the primary source of technical information on the design, construction, and maintenance, use of highways, roads, and other transportation facilities. AASHTO is the only national organization recognized by the Federal Highway Administration whose interests include all of the transportation modes, including bicycling. They have identified ten safety issues for consideration when a bicycle path uses the same right-of-way (ROW) as vehicular traffic.

1. **Width**: Bicycle paths on paved roadway without parking should have their own exclusive ROWs with striping to separate them from automobile traffic. Paths should be 4 feet wide and allow for a two-foot wide shoulder at the roadways edge. If parking is allowed on the side of the roadway, the parking should be ten feet wide from the inside of the shoulder with a striped five foot bicycle path, abutting the roadway. Bicycle paths should never be placed on sidewalks.
2. **One-way paths**: On two-way streets, bicycle paths should be provided on both sides of the street, to the right of the right-most through lane. Under no condition should a two-way lane be provided on one side of a roadway.
3. **Side of the road**: On one-way streets, a one way lane should be generally be provided on the right side of the road. There may be special instances that dictate striping a lane on the left side of the roadway but this should be given careful thought.
4. **Designation**: Bicycle paths should be designated by lane striping, regulatory signs, and pavement markings determined by local authorities' rules on signage.
5. **Striping**: Bicycle paths should be separated from other travel lanes by a 6-inch to 8-inch solid white stripe.
6. **Regulatory Signage**: Signage to identify bicycle routes, especially at intersections, should be used.
7. **Pavement Markings**: Pavement markings are an alternative to regulatory signage and to minimize the aesthetic impact of signage on the environment.
8. **Intersections**: Depending on the level of use of an intersection, simple striping of the bicycle lane can be used in most cases with signage or pavement markings to help direct the bicyclist in the right direction.
9. **Parking**: Parking should be to the traffic side of all curb-side or parallel parking locations. The standard width for parking is between 8 and ten feet and should not be narrowed to accommodate a bicycle lane. Diagonal parking does not work well with lanes and should be avoided if possible.
10. **Signals**: If a traffic-actuated signal is to be included, special accommodations should be made to allow them to be detected and synchronized with the turning movements of vehicles.

6.1.3 Issues

The major issues for consideration in planning for bicycle paths in and around Schoodic Peninsula are:

*   None of the roadways or bicycle routes in the study area currently complies with AASHTO guidelines. Each of the six roadway segments need improvements to at least approach AASHTO safety guidelines.
*   Coordination among all stakeholding governmental bodies, namely the Park Service, the State of Maine, and the towns of Winter Harbor and Gouldsboro, for identifying funding options, prioritizing projects, and the proper planning and phasing of construction work.
*   The third issue is the proposed designation of the National Park on Schoodic Peninsula as a National Resource District, which would identify the park road as an historic feature with a high level of integrity. If the designation occurs, any

modifications to the roadway would have to adhere to the guidelines established by the Interior Department's Standards for the Treatment of Historic Properties and the Guidelines for the Treatment of Cultural Landscapes (IDS-HPGTCL).

- Planners must take both the short term and long term views of bicycle access planning. All of the bicycle routes in this study have ROWs following pre-existing paved roadways, dictating the development of bicycle routes in the short term. Long term expansion of opportunities for bicyclists may mean acquiring private ROWs or easements. a potentially difficult process.

6.1.4 Integration with other projects and studies

Several studies and transportation improvement initiatives by stakeholders affect bicycle route planning and will require effective coordination. The State of Maine's document "Examination of Tourism in Maine: Its Economic Impact and Marketing" (April 2001) should be revised to include Schoodic bicycle route planning. The State's roads maintenance plan must include improvements for bicycle routes to minimize the effort and costs associated with the work.

Any work that the Park Service performs should consider the roadway as a historic feature due to the IDS-HPGTCL and be planned to minimize impact on historic features of the area.

Two studies by the HCPC examine transportation planning for Schoodic Peninsula. The first was a grant application to the FHWA's National Scenic Byways Program for pedestrian and bicycle access improvements for the Schoodic Byway. Therein, HCPC identified several sections of roadway in need of a bicycle lane and other safety measures and estimated costs for design, construction, and implementation. Secondly, the HCPC produced a draft report by the Pedestrian Subcommittee for the Region Two Transportation Advisory Committee in September of 2000 in response to a new regional plan under development by the Maine Department of Transportation. This report identifies priorities for shoulder paving in Hancock and Washington Counties.

The towns of Winter Harbor and Gouldsboro are both in the process of updating their Comprehensive Plans, which include identification of opportunities for improving pedestrian and bicycle access and mention of the possibilities for acquiring new ROWs or easements for bicycle paths parallel to the roadways. This is would be part of a long-term bicycle transportation plan in the area.

6.2 Demand

The demand for bicycle transportation in Schoodic Peninsula is the proportion of visitors indicating in surveys that they rode or would ride bicycles in Acadia National Park multiplied by the projected visitation numbers for Schoodic for the various Transportation Alternatives. The 1998 Mount Desert Island survey (Littlejohn) indicated that 36% of visitors there used bicycles, while the 2000 survey work by University of Vermont in Schoodic found 17% did. A range is chosen here with a minimum of 17% and a maximum splitting the difference between the two survey values, or 26%. In the latter case, transportation systems improvements may be expected to enhance demand, but would probably not elevate it to the levels seen on MDI where bicycling opportunities are much better.

6.2.1 Transportation Alternative 2

The seasonal demand for bicycle use is a function of total recreational trips. Table 6-2 presents the total numbers of bicyclists for each year and Reuse Concept. Between 5% and 6% of the bicycle trips for all scenarios would be people arriving by bus in the bus service only Alternative.

6.2.2 Transportation Alternative 3

The seasonal demand for bicycle use is a function of total recreational trips. The demand calculation includes the assumptions that Alternative 3 would provide the visitor free access for bicycles on the ferry or bus and that there would be no constraint on parking for those who wish to bring their bicycles with their vehicles. The results of the demand analysis appear in Table 6-2, which shows that the bicycle trips would range from a low of 35,200 in the 2005 Low Reuse scenario to a maximum of 48,300 in the 2015 High Reuse scenario.

| Year | Base Reuse | Bicycle Usage | Annual Trips | | | | | |
| | | | Recreational Visits | Bicycle Trips | Alt. 2 (Bus) Bicycle | | Alt. 3 (Ferry) Bicycle | |
					Auto	Bus	Auto	Ferry
2005	Concept 3, High	26%	255,031	66,308	62,330	3,978	61,666	4,642
	Concept 3, High	17%	255,031	43,355	40,754	2,601	40,320	3,035
	Concept 1, Low	26%	207,342	53,909	51,213	2,695	50,674	3,235
	Concept 1, Low	17%	207,342	35,248	33,486	1,762	33,133	2,115
2015	Concept 3, High	26%	284,379	73,939	69,502	4,436	68,763	5,176
	Concept 3, High	17%	284,379	48,344	45,444	2,901	44,960	3,384
	Concept 1, Low	26%	235,024	61,106	58,051	3,055	57,440	3,666
	Concept 1, Low	17%	235,024	39,954	37,956	1,998	37,557	2,397

Table 6-2
Alternative 3 Seasonal Bicycle Trips

6.2.3 Transportation Alternative 4

Alternative 4 would result in a marginally small increase in bicycle trips for all scenarios relative to Alternative 3 (a range of 5 - 7 % higher), due to recreational users from the ferry during the off-season. Most bicycle use will occur during the May to October seasonal ferry and bus loop service provided by Alternative 3.

6.3 Schoodic Loop Road

The following discussion of reconfiguration options for the Schoodic Loop Road is on the assumption that there is no expansion (i.e., widening) of the roadway in any case because of the pending designation of the Schoodic parkland as a National Resource District because of its historic value.

6.3.1 Current conditions and options

Bicyclists touring Schoodic generally follow the loop as dictated by the direction of the one-way Park road, i.e., west to east (Winter Harbor to Birch Harbor, then back to Winter Harbor). The following options explore ways in which the Park roads could be modified through directional changes and application of modern design criteria to provide the safest bicycle route.

6.3.2 One-way option

This option would reconfigure the two-lane Park road to one lane for vehicular traffic, a wide bicycle lane, and an extended shoulder running south from Frazer Point to Schoodic Point Road, then turning north towards Birch Harbor. This option would limit the bicyclist to one direction of movement and require completion of the 12-mile loop. It provides the maximum width for a bicycle lane on the right side of the roadway without expanding the existing roadway and would preserve the historic configuration and character of the road.

6.3.3 Two-way option

This approach would reconfigure the loop road to a two-way road with direct access from the Winter Harbor and Birch Harbor sides. Each lane on the roadway would be only about 10 feet wide, inadequate by current AASHTO standards, with two foot wide gravel shoulders. There would be no opportunity to incorporate a bicycle lane without widening the road and removing numerous copingstones and several rock outcroppings, all actions inimical to the intent of IDS-HPGTCL for National Resource Districts. Such an expansion would not allow even soft shoulders on both sides for bicycle use and would therefore limiting bicyclists to one direction, probably west to east. This option provides more benefit for vehicular traffic than for bicyclists and is not a viable course of action from the standpoint of the bicycling mode.

6.3.4 One way / two way option

This concept includes the retention of the one-way road from Frazer Point to Schoodic Point Road, with the integration of a bicycle path, and the reconfiguration of the Park road from Schoodic Point Road to Birch Harbor for two-way vehicular traffic. The roadway from Schoodic Point to Birch Harbor would not meet AASHTO guidelines and it would be difficult to have any bicycle lane with changing the character of the roadway. Moore Road up to the Schoodic Point Road would have an improved bicycle path without having to expand.

These changes would provide the benefit of a two-lane road for cars on one portion of the road and the benefit of improved bicycle access on another, a "neither fish nor fowl" result failing to improve transport by either mode. On balance, the benefits would favor motorists rather than bicyclists and would not be a desirable option.

6.3.5 Two way / one way option

This concept is the mirror image of the previous approach and would have the same problems. The road from Frazer Point to Schoodic Point would be reconfigured for two-way traffic. Expanded width would be unlikely because of the necessity to remove copingstones; therefore a bicycle lane to Winter Harbor could not be included. The road to Birch Harbor would have improved bicycle access without any expansion but would be limited by its short two-way portion just before the Park exit.

6.3.6 Schoodic Loop Road

This section is currently a two-way spur road and needs to be maintained as such for access to the Navy base entrance and the Schoodic Point Visitor Area. It is narrow and has some exposed ledge protruding out over the shoulder near the parking lot. This section should have its shoulders widened to accommodate a bicycle lane on either side of the roadway.

6.3.7 Conclusion

The goal of providing a safe bicycle route through the Schoodic parkland, one that adheres to AASHTO guidelines, is best attained by retaining the one-way loop configuration from Frazer Point to the Park exit at Birch Harbor and reassigning the existing lanes as follows: one lane for vehicular traffic, and the seaward lane for 5' wide bicycle lane and a 5' extended shoulder. Striping, signage, and pavement markings are important elements of the conversion that would have minimal impact on the roadway. Some restriction of traffic flow would occur at peak periods, but the effect would be mitigated by promoting the use of the park-and-ride lots, ferries, and buses and reducing automobile traffic. Otherwise, expansion of the roadway's width would be required for a bicycle path, whether for two lane, one-way or two lane, two-way automobile traffic configuration. The latter choice depends on the outcome of the road's designation as part of an historic district.

The Schoodic Point spur road must continue as a two way vehicular way. The recommendation for bicycle lanes on both sides means that this would be the one area requiring road surface expansion. This would be a small proportion of the total length of roads in the Schoodic parkland.

6.4 Gouldsboro and Winter Harbor Roads

6.4.1 Moore Road, Winter Harbor

This section of roadway should have the gravel shoulders replaced with pavement. A couple of ledge outcroppings near the shoulders should be removed. Lane striping and signage should be added.

6.4.2 Route 186, Winter Harbor to Birch Harbor

This section of roadway needs paved shoulders, lane striping and signage. The Regional Transportation Advisory Committee considered this road a safety priority due to its heavy seasonal use. SR 186 has the largest daily volume of traffic and also the fastest average speed. This stretch of narrow, relatively high speed roadway has some rolling hills and curves and poses added danger to bicyclists and pedestrians.

6.4.3 Schoodic Road, Gouldsboro

This section of roadway has very narrow shoulders that need to be expanded by 2 to 3 feet on either side to accommodate a bi-directional four-foot bicycle lane. Lane striping and signage should be added to direct the bicyclist along the route. There may be some problems expanding the roadway due to the proximity of people's yards to the shoulder. This may require easements or acquiring a 2 to 4 foot ROW along either side of the roadway.

6.5 Park and Ride Opportunities

6.5.1 Ferry service

The ferry service should be inter-modal, allowing people to get and use bicycles at either end of the trip. For commuters, a bicycle rack should be made available at the Winter Harbor Dock and at the terminal in Bar Harbor. For recreational trips, bicycles should be allowed on the ferry or be available from rentals near the Winter Harbor Town Center Lot or the marina dock. Signage or bicycle route maps should be readily available to the bicyclist as well as the local schedules.

6.5.2 Bus and automobile

People who visit the Schoodic parkland in their cars should have the option of using a park-and-ride lot in central Winter Harbor and transferring to loop bus service or bicycles. It has been suggested that a park-and-ride lot is an appropriate use at the site of the Navy's Misty Harbor Apartments, which are to be turned over to the Town of Winter Harbor. Such a conversion would require bicycle racks, as well as a variable message sign in Winter Harbor as you approach Main Street with information on loop road traffic and limited parking inside the Schoodic parkland. Motorists would thus be encouraged to use the park-and-ride lot at peak times.

7 BUS SERVICES

Bus services would play critical roles in each of the three active Transportation
Alternative, both to link the Schoodic Peninsula and Mount Desert Island and to provide
local transit at either end. Two distinct services are described:

1. Between Bar Harbor and Schoodic Peninsula, with five, six, or seven daily
   roundtrips. The services described would be 1) the sole year round inter-regional
   transit option under Alternative 2, 2) the sole off-season (November - April) inter-
   regional transit option under Alternative 3; and 3) the back-up service for the year
   round ferry under Alternative 4.
2. Connecting loop service from the Winter Harbor terminal, rather bus or ferry, to
   other Schoodic Point stops, and service between the Bar Harbor terminal to
   major MDI employers and other bus lines on MDI (Alternatives 2, 3, and 4).

Each service description addresses the needs of multiple markets, as described in
Chapter 3.

Commuter markets will require year-round weekday service for all active Alternatives.
Midday links for staff and program participants are likely to be needed on a regular five-
day-a-week basis, although it would be possible to limit midday transportation to special
occasions. Evening trips would likely be offered only on days when special conference
outings are planned.

The need for weekend service will depend in part on whether weekend conferences are
planned at Schoodic Point, and in part on whether seasonal tourist traffic will be great
enough to justify seasonal weekend operations. There is unlikely to be sufficient
demand for weekend commuter service.

Recreational use of the bus service between Bar Harbor and Schoodic Peninsula by
Park visitors would occur for those Alternatives lacking ferry service either year round or
seasonally and in those instances when ferry service is not available (maintenance and
repairs, weather cancellations). It is likely, however, that this recreational demand in
any of those cases will be less than demand for ferry service, given the visitor
experience value of a ferry ride. Discussion of markets and services in this chapter
therefore focuses on non-recreational users, i.e., commuters, Park staff, and staff,
researchers, and guests at the future facilities on the Navy base.

7.1 Bar Harbor to Schoodic Service

"Bus only" service between Bar Harbor and Schoodic Peninsula would address a variety
of possible scenarios under the active Transportation Alternatives:

- Ferry service fails to start up or fails to succeed once started due to economic,
  operational, or infrastructure issues.
- Buses replace seasonal service ferries during off-season months.
- Buses operate as back-ups to ferry service on individual days when ferries
  cannot operate due to weather or sea conditions, or repair and maintenance
  needs.

7.1.1 Bus Only – Level One

"Level One " service would provide two buses for limited commuter and midday links between the Schoodic Peninsula and Bar Harbor. One 35 or 40 passenger bus would be based on the Schoodic peninsula and offer four daily roundtrips. A second smaller bus would be based in Winter Harbor overnight and would remain at the Jackson Laboratory during the day. The second bus would offer a single run from Winter Harbor to Bar Harbor in the morning and a single return trip in the late afternoon.

A draft schedule for this limited "bus only" service is presented in Table 7-1. A description of how target markets would be accommodated is presented in Table 7-2.

Schoodic	Winter Harbor	ANP	Bar Harbor	Jackson Lab	Jackson Lab	Bar Harbor	ANP	Winter Harbor	Schoodic
5:30 a	5:45 a	6:45 a	6:55 a	7:00 a	7:05 a	7:10 a	7:20 a	8:20 a	8:35 a
7:00 a	7:15 a	8:15 a	8:25 a	8:30 a					
9:00 a	9:15 a	10:15 a	10:25 a	10:30 a	10:35 a	10:40 a	10:50 a	11:50 a	12:05 p
2:00 p	2:15 p	3:15 p	3:25 p	3:30 p	3:35 p	3:40 p	3:50 p	4:50 p	5:05 p
					5:05 p	5:10 p	5:20 p	6:20 p	6:35 p
5:15 p	5:30 p	-	6:40 p	-	-	*6:40 p	-	7:50 p	8:05 p
						*8:00 p	-	9:10 p	9:25 p

*Optional late returns to accommodate conference attendees

Table 7-1
Schedule - Level One Bus Service

This service plan assumes that the driver of the second bus would be employed during the day at the Jackson Laboratory, avoiding the cost of "deadhead" runs in the morning and afternoon. The proposed schedule has this driver arriving at the Laboratory at 8:35 a.m. and departing at 5:15 p.m. These times could be shifted to match commuter demand.

A medium-duty 28-passenger bus could be used for the dedicated Jackson Laboratory run. The remainder of the service should be provided using comfortable, heavy-duty equipment. The best approach would be to utilize a new or used 40-passenger motorcoach. While this equipment is more expensive, it is very durable and reliable, and it will ensure the highest level of comfort for commuters, staff, and Park program participants.

The Level One service would involve approximately 15.5 vehicle service hours per day. The first bus would operate approximately 6.5 hours in the morning and 6 hours in the afternoon, with a 2-hour midday break. The second bus would operate approximately 1.5 hours in the morning and 1.5 hours in the afternoon. Evening service will add roughly 1.5 to 2 hours for each day it is provided.

Market	Available options	Comments
Jackson Lab commuters	Arrive at the Laboratory at 7:00 a.m. and 8:30 a.m. Depart the Laboratory at 3:35 p.m. and 5:05 p.m.	This serves the main 7:30 a.m. – 3:30 p.m. shift, while also accommodating administrators and scientists who work past 3:30 p.m.
MDI residents employed at Schoodic	Arrive at the new ANP facility at 8:35 a.m. and depart at 5:15 p.m.	
Attendees at midday meetings on Schoodic	Arrive at Schoodic at 8:35 a.m. or 12:05 p.m. Depart Schoodic at 2:00 p.m. or 5:15 p.m.	The shortest available midday stay would be 4.5 hours.
Attendees at midday meetings on MDI	Arrive at ANP headquarters at 8:15 a.m., 10:15 a.m., or 3:15 p.m. Depart at 10:50 a.m., 3:50 p.m., or 5:20 p.m.	Accommodates midday stays of 2.5 and 5.5 hours.
Evening trips to Bar Harbor to serve conference attendees	Arrive in Bar Harbor at 3:25 p.m. or 6:40 p.m. Depart Bar Harbor at 8:00 p.m.	This would involve holding the 6:40 p.m. "deadhead" bus in Bar Harbor until 8:00 p.m. The departure time could be customized for particular groups.

Table 7-2
Markets Served, Level One Bus Service

Downeast Transportation, Inc. (DTI), the public transit provider for Hancock County, would be the likely operator of Bar Harbor-Schoodic bus service. DTI's current operating cost is $25 per service hour. With this unit cost, the cost of year-round weekday service would total approximately $96,875. Evening runs would cost an additional $40-50 per day. If thirty evening conference trips are scheduled, the additional cost would be between $1,200 and $1,500.

There are a number of options for reducing the scope and cost of Level One service. It would be possible to omit the scheduled midday 9:00 a.m. to 12:05 p.m. roundtrip, holding the bus in reserve for special trips instead on an as needed basis. It would also be possible to do without the extra Jackson Laboratory bus, relying on just the 7:00 a.m. arrival and the 3:35 p.m. departure. Each of these changes would save roughly three hours each day, or roughly $18,750 each per year.

If only one Jackson Lab commute trip is offered, this will likely limit the usefulness of the transportation service for many Laboratory employees. In addition to serving a later work shift, the later run provides a back up for earlier workers who sometimes need to work past 3:30 p.m.

7.1.2 Bus Only – Level Two

A more intensive "bus only" service would use two regularly scheduled buses, one based on Schoodic Peninsula and the other based in Bar Harbor. The schedule presented in Table 7-3 includes a total of six weekday roundtrips, plus an optional evening roundtrip. The bus based on Schoodic would offer a single morning roundtrip and a single afternoon roundtrip, plus the optional evening service. The Bar Harbor bus would offer two morning roundtrips, one midday roundtrip, and one late afternoon roundtrip. This service plan would accommodate markets as described in Table 7-4.

Schoodic	Winter Harbor	ANP	Bar Harbor	Jackson Lab	Schoodic	Winter Harbor	ANP	Bar Harbor	Jackson Lab
					5:30 a	5:35 a	5:45 a	6:45 a	7:00 a
5:30 a	5:45 a	6:45 a	6:55 a	7:00 a	7:05 a	7:10 a	7:20 a	8:20 a	8:35 a
7:05 a	7:20 a	8:20 a	8:30 a	8:35 a	8:50 a	8:55 a	9:05 a	10:05 a	10:20 a
10:30 a	10:45 a	11:45 a	11:55 a	12:00 p	12:05 p	12:10 p	12:20 p	1:20 p	1:35 p
1:45 p	2:00 p	3:00 p	3:10 p	3:15 p					
					3:35 p	3:40 p	3:50 p	4:50 p	5:05 p
3:30 p	3:45 p	4:45 p	4:55 p	5:00 p	5:05 p	5:10 p	5:20 p	6:20 p	6:35 p
5:10 p	5:25 p	-	6:35 p	6:40 p					
*6:40 p	6:55 p	-	8:05 p	-	-	8:15 p	-	9:25 p	9:40 p

*Optional evening run to accommodate conference attendees

Table 7-3
Schedule - Level Two Bus Service

This service could be provided using two 35 or 40 passenger buses. The best strategy would be to use heavy-duty motorcoach equipment to ensure maximum reliability and passenger comfort.

This alternative would involve a total of roughly 20 hours per day, plus an additional 3 hours per day when evening runs are scheduled. One bus would operate just over 13 hours a day, from 5:30 a.m. until 6:40 p.m. This would require two drivers, one working an 8-hour shift and another working a 5-hour shift. The second bus would require a split shift of three hours in the morning and three hours in the afternoon, plus an additional 3 hours when evenings runs are scheduled.

At $25 per hour, this level 2 bus only service will cost approximately $125,000 per year for regular weekday service. Extra evening runs will cost about $75 per day, or $2,250 for 30 evening runs per year.

Market	Available options	Comments
Jackson Lab commuters	Arrive at the Laboratory at 7:00 a.m. and 8:35 a.m. Depart the Laboratory at 3:35 p.m. and 5:05 p.m.	This is similar to the Level 1 option. It serves the main 7:30 a.m. – 3:30 p.m. shift, plus administrators and scientists who start later or who work until 5:00 p.m.
MDI residents employed at Schoodic	Arrive at the new ANP facility at 7:00 a.m. and 8:35 a.m. Depart at 3:30 p.m. and 5:10 p.m.	This alternative provides better commuter links for the new ANP research facility. It serves both a 7:00 a.m. to 3:30 p.m. shift and a 8:30 a.m. to 5:00 p.m. shift.
Attendees at midday meetings on Schoodic	Arrive at Schoodic at 8:35 a.m., 10:20 a.m., or 1:35 p.m. Depart Schoodic at 10:30 a.m., 1:45 p.m., 3:30 p.m., or 5:15 p.m.	This option provides a better choice of midday stays at Schoodic.
Attendees at midday meetings on MDI	Arrive at ANP headquarters at 8:20 a.m., 11:45 a.m., or 3:00 p.m. Depart at 12:20 p.m.., 3:50 p.m., or 5:20 p.m.	This option also provides a better choice of midday stays in Bar Harbor.
Evening trips to Bar Harbor to accommodate conference attendees	Arrive in Bar Harbor at 3:10 p.m., 4:55 p.m., or 6:35 p.m. Depart Bar Harbor at 8:15 p.m.	This involves a separate evening roundtrip. The departure time from Bar Harbor can be later to suit the needs of individual groups.

Table 7-4
Markets Served, Level Two Bus Service

7.2 Bus Links for Ferry Alternatives

If ferry service is provided between Bar Harbor and Winter Harbor, two different connecting bus services will be required:

- Service from the Winter Harbor terminal to Schoodic Point and other points on the Peninsula be needed to accommodate commuters from Bar Harbor, Park Service staff and others traveling to and from the new research facility, and seasonal visitors traveling from Bar Harbor to the Schoodic portion of Acadia National Park.
- Service between the Bar Harbor terminal to major employers and other points in Bar Harbor to accommodate commuter and recreational ferry passengers arriving in Bar Harbor.

Additional markets could be served, although it may prove difficult to accomplish this with a single bus at each end of the ferry route. Other potential bus links include:

- Midday buses between the Bar Harbor town pier and Acadia National Park headquarters.
- A bus from Winter Harbor to Corea for MDI residents commuting to jobs at the former Navy facility.
- A commuter bus from Milbridge to Winter Harbor for Washington County residents employed at Jackson Lab.
- A more extensive visitor shuttle serving a small number of tourist destinations located north of Prospect Harbor.

While these extra services have been considered during the planning process, detailed schedules and service plans have not been developed for these markets.

7.2.1 Bus /Ferry Links: Bar Harbor and Schoodic Peninsula

The schedule and frequency of connecting bus service on both sides of Frenchman's Bay depends on the schedule and frequency of ferry service. The ferry and bus schedules have been designed around a 25 minute voyage time between Bar Harbor and Winter Harbor (one monohull service, Chapter 5) and a minimum layover time of 10 minutes between ferry runs. The one monohull schedule developed has uniform layover times of 15 minutes or more.

These ferry schedules result in a total of at least 80 minutes between roundtrip ferry departures. This results in a window of approximately 90 minutes within which a Schoodic bus can distribute arriving ferry passengers and pick up new riders for delivery to the ferry terminal. At least five factors need to be considered in developing coordinated schedules at both ends of the ferry route:

(1) The amount of time required for a bus to travel around the Schoodic Peninsula.
(2) Desired arrival and departure times for people commuting to jobs at Schoodic Point.
(3) The amount of time required for a bus to link the Bar Harbor town pier with the Jackson Laboratory.
(4) Major shift changes at Jackson Laboratory and desired arrival and departure times.
(5) The need to minimize disruption of non-ferry users of an in-town Bar Harbor-Jackson Lab shuttle bus.

A number of desired features should be included, if possible, in a set of coordinated bus and ferry timetables:

- Jackson Laboratory employees should be able to arrive at the Bar Harbor town pier and transfer directly to a waiting bus for a six-minute ride to the Laboratory. The main Laboratory work shift begins at 7:30 a.m., and most workers prefer to arrive by about 7:10 a.m.
- Other Laboratory commuters should be able to arrive for shifts that begin at 6:00 a.m. and 8:30 a.m.
- Laboratory workers should be able to board buses there when their shift ends and travel directly to the town pier for direct transfers to a departing ferry.
- Bus runs between the Laboratory and the town pier should cause minimal disruption of Bar Harbor village shuttles for bus riders who do not use the ferry.

This is important to avoid the cost of operating a separate bus for just three morning and three afternoon ferry runs.

- MDI residents employed at Schoodic Point should be able to get off the ferry and board a bus at the Winter Harbor dock for direct rides to the new Acadia National Park research facility.
- A bus should be waiting for Schoodic Point workers at the end of the workday to return them to a ferry waiting in Winter Harbor.
- ANP staff and program participants should be able to transfer directly between ferries and buses in Winter Harbor for travel to and from the new Schoodic Point research facility.
- Seasonal visitors should be able ride the ferry from Bar Harbor to Winter Harbor and then transfer to a bus that would take them to destinations in the Schoodic area of Acadia National Park.
- Bus schedules should provide visitors with convenient options for visiting Winter Harbor's village center.
- Buses should transport bicycles, allowing cyclists to limit their biking to the one-way portion of the Schoodic road.
- Buses in Winter Harbor should serve major in-town residential subdivisions, providing Winter Harbor residents with car-free access to the ferry dock.
- Buses operating between Winter Harbor and Schoodic Point should provide a transportation link for local residents employed at the new ANP Schoodic facility

Because a roundtrip circuit of the Schoodic peninsula can be completed in 45 minutes, it should be possible, if necessary, for buses to offer two complete round trips between the arrival of a ferry and a subsequent departure. In-town stops on these runs may need to be limited to ensure that there is enough time to complete both runs.

To maximize benefits for groups traveling in both directions, it will be necessary in some instances for a bus to deliver passengers to a departing ferry, while also picking up ferry passengers that have just arrived.

One possible scheduling solution is presented in Table 7-5. This draft schedule shows times for a Schoodic bus, Winter Harbor-Bar Harbor ferries, and a bus link between the Bar Harbor town pier and Jackson Laboratory. A summary of markets served appears in Table 7-6. The Bar Harbor in-town shuttle schedule appears in Table 7-7.

The draft schedule of Table 7-5 includes nine ferry round trips:

- Three roundtrips between 5:15 a.m. and 9:00 a.m., followed by a 60 minute layover.
- Two roundtrips between 10:00 a.m. and 12:40 p.m., followed by a 50 minute layover.
- Three roundtrips between 1:30 p.m. and 6:40 p.m..

During commute hours, ferry times are determined mostly by Jackson Laboratory shift changes. Midday ferry times are affected by the need to allow convenient transfer times to and from buses traveling the Schoodic loop.

Table 7-5

Integrated Bar Harbor-Schoodic Bus and Ferry Schedule

Column groups (left to right): **BUS** (Jax Lab, B. Hbr. Dock) · **FERRY** (Ferry to Winter Harbor) · **BUS** — Winter Harbor loop (W. Hbr. Marina, W. Hbr. IGA, Frazier Point, Navy Base, Schoodic Point, Birch Harbor, Prospect Harbor, IGA, W. Hbr. Marina) · **FERRY** (Ferry to Bar Harbor) · **BUS** (Bar Harbor, Jax Lab)

Jax Lab	B. Hbr. Dock	Ferry to Winter Harbor	W. Hbr. Marina	W. Hbr. IGA	Frazier Point	Navy Base	Schoodic Point	Birch Harbor	Prospect Harbor	IGA	W. Hbr. Marina	Ferry to Bar Harbor	Bar Harbor	Jax Lab
										6:21 a *	6:25 a #	5:15 a / 5:42 a	5:45 a	5:51 a
		5:55 a / 6:22 a	6:25 a	6:27 a –	–	6:40 a	–	6:50 a	6:55 a	7:00 a	7:05 a #	6:35 a / 7:02 a	7:05 a	7:11 a
		7:15 a / 7:42 a	7:45 a	7:47 a –	–	8:00 a	–	8:10 a	8:15 a	7:41 a *	7:45 a #	7:52 a / 8:19 a	8:22 a	8:28 a
		8:30 a / 8:57 a	9:00 a	9:02 a #	9:10 a	9:18 a	9:20 a	9:30 a	9:35 a	8:20 a	8:25 a #			
			10:20 a	10:22 a #	10:30 a	10:38 a	10:40 a	10:50 a	10:55 a	9:40 a	9:45 a #	10:00 a / 10:27 a		
		10:40 a / 11:07 a	11:10 a	11:12 a #	11:20 a	11:28 a	11:30 a	11:40 a	11:45 a	11:00 a	11:05 a #	11:20 a / 11:47 a		
		12:10 p / 12:37 p	12:40 p	12:42 p #	12:50 p	12:58 p	1:00 p	1:10 p	1:15 p	11:50 a	11:55 a #			
			1:45 p	1:47 p #	1:55 p	2:03 p	2:05 p	2:15 p	2:20 p	1:20 p	1:25 p #	1:30 p / 1:57 p		
2:00 p	2:06 p	2:10 p / 2:37 p	2:40 p *	2:46 p #	2:55 p	3:03 p	3:05 p	3:15 p		2:25 p	2:30 p #	2:50 p / 3:17 p		
			3:30 p	3:32 p #	3:40 p	3:50 p		4:00 p		3:20 p	3:25 p #			
3:30 p	3:36 p	3:40 p / 4:07 p	4:10 p *	4:16 p #		4:30 p		4:40 p		4:05 p	4:07 p –	4:20 p / 4:47 p		
			4:54 p			5:10 p		5:20 p		4:49 p *	4:54 p #			
4:49 a	4:55 a	5:00 p / 5:27 p	5:35 p *	5:41 p #						5:29 p *	5:34 p #	5:40 p / 6:07 p		
		6:10 p / 6:37 p												
		8:00 p / 8:27 p												

Optional evening ferry run when conferences are scheduled

* Includes stops at former Navy housing complexes in Winter Harbor.

\# Operates via Bar Harbor Banking and Trust on Main Street, Winter Harbor.

Market	Available options	Comments
Jackson Lab commuters	Arrive at the Laboratory at 5:51 a.m., 7:11 a.m., and 8:28 a.m. Depart the Laboratory at 2:00 p.m., 3:30 p.m., and 4:49 p.m.	Serves three shifts: 6:00 a.m. – 2:00 p.m. 7:30 a.m. – 3:30 p.m. 8:30 a.m. – 4:45 p.m.
MDI residents employed at Schoodic	Arrive at the new ANP facility at 6:40 a.m., 8:00 a.m., and 9:18 a.m. Depart at 2:03 p.m., 3:50 p.m., and 5:10 p.m.	Serves a variety of possible work hours: 6:40 a.m. – 2:03 or 3:50 p.m. 8:00 a.m. – 3:50 or 5:10 p.m. 9:18 a.m. – 5:10 p.m.
Attendees at midday meetings on Schoodic	Arrive at Schoodic at 9:18 a.m., 11:28 a.m., 12:58 p.m., or 3:03 p.m. Depart Schoodic at 10:38 a.m., 12:58 p.m., 2:03 p.m., 3:50 p.m., or 5:10 p.m.	Provides a wide selection of midday stays at Schoodic.
Attendees at midday meetings on MDI	Arrive in Bar Harbor at 10:27 a.m., 11:47 a.m., 1:57 p.m., or 3:17 p.m. Depart at Bar Harbor 12:10 p.m.., 2:10 p.m., 3:40 p.m., or 5:00 p.m.	Provides a choice of midday stays in Bar Harbor. A midday bus may be needed for rides between the Bar Harbor town pier and ANP headquarters.
Evening trips to Bar Harbor to accommodate conference attendees	Arrive in Bar Harbor at 2:50 p.m., 4:20 p.m., or 5:40 p.m. Depart Bar Harbor at 8:00 p.m.	Involves holding the 6:10 p.m. deadhead ferry departure from Bar Harbor. The departure time from Bar Harbor can be set to suit the needs of individual groups.

Table 7- 6
Markets Served - Coordinated Bus and Ferry Schedules

7.2.1.1 Schoodic bus schedules

The Schoodic bus schedule includes eleven trips around the Schoodic peninsula. Schedules call for eleven hours of bus service each day, with a six-hour shift running from 6:21 a.m. until 9:45 a.m., and a 5-hour shift running from 12:40 p.m. until 5:40 p.m. Most Schoodic bus runs are scheduled to depart the Winter Harbor ferry terminal within three minutes of the arriving ferry. In most cases, buses are scheduled to arrive at the Winter Harbor dock 15 minutes before ferries are scheduled to depart. The exceptions are the two afternoon commuter connections, with transfer times of 13 and 6 minutes.

During commute hours, buses include stops at former Navy housing complexes in Winter Harbor. All bus runs include stops at the Winter Harbor IGA. Most runs also serve Main Street in Winter Harbor, with a turn at the Bar Harbor Banking and Trust building. Early morning and midday bus runs have sufficient time to include stops in Prospect Harbor after they exit Acadia National Park and before they arrive back in Winter Harbor. Afternoon commuter runs bypass Prospect Harbor.

MORNING SERVICE									
Jackson Lab	Store	Pier	Ledge-lawn	COA	West St. Ext.	Ledge-lawn	Pier	Store	Jackson Lab
				5:36 a	5:41 a	-	5:45 a	5:48 a	5:51 a
6:00 a	6:03 a	-	6:05 a	6:10 a	6:15 a	6:17 a	-	6:20 a	6:23 a
6:30 a	6:33 a	-	6:35 a	6:40 a	6:45 a	6:47 a	-	6:50 a	6:53 a
6:55 a	-	7:00 a	-	-	-	-	7:05 a	7:08 a	7:11 a
7:15 a	7:18 a	-	7:20 a	7:25 a	7:30 a	7:32 a	-	7:35 a	7:38 a
7:45 a	7:48 a	-	7:50 a	7:55 a	8:00 a	8:02 a	-	8:05 a	8:08 a
8:10 a		8:15 a	-	-	-	-	8:22 a	8:25 a	8:28 a
8:30 a	8:33 a	-	8:35 a	8:40 a	8:45 a	8:47 a	-	8:50 a	8:53 a
9:00 a	9:03 a	-	9:05 a	9:10 a					

AFTERNOON SERVICE									
Jackson Lab	Store	Pier	Ledgelawn	COA	West St. Ext.	Ledgelawn	Pier	Store	Jackson Lab
2:00 p	2:03 p	2:06 p	-	-	-	-	2:06 p	-	2:12 p
2:15 p	2:18 p	-	2:20 p	2:25 p	2:30 p	2:32 p	-	2:35 p	2:38 p
2:45 p	2:48 p	-	2:50 p	2:55 p	3:00 p	3:02 p	-	3:05 p	3:08 p
3:30 p	3:33 p	3:36 p	-	-	-	-	3:36 p	-	3:42 p
3:45 p	3:48 p	-	3:50 p	3:55 p	4:00 p	4:02 p	-	4:05 p	4:08 p
4:15 p	4:18 p	-	4:20 p	4:25 p	4:30 p	4:32 p	-	4:35 p	4:38 p
4:49 p	4:52 p	4:55 p	-	-	-	-	4:55 p	-	5:01 p
5:05 p	5:08 p	-	5:10 p	5:15 p	5:20 p	5:22 p	-	5:25 p	5:28 p
5:35 p	5:38 p	-	5:40 p	5:45 p	5:50 p	5:52 p	-	5:55 p	5:58 p
6:05 p	6:08 p	-	6:10 p	6:15 p	6:20 p	6:22 p			

Table 7-7
Bar Harbor-Jackson Lab Village Shuttle Schedule

There does not appear to be sufficient time to offer commuter bus links to Corea or Milbridge using just one bus. A separate bus designed to transport Jackson Lab commuters from Milbridge to the Winter Harbor ferry dock could perhaps also be scheduled to provide a commuter link between Winter Harbor and a potential future job site in Corea.

If a Schoodic bus operates year-round on weekdays only, this should result in an estimated 2,750 annual service hours. At $25 an hour, the cost for operations should total approximately $68,750 per year. If weekend service is offered seven hours per day for six months, this will add another 364 hours of service, at an estimated cost of $9,100 per year.

A bus like the 28-passenger Island Explorer buses would likely be suitable for Winter Harbor-Schoodic bus service. Assuming that it would be operated by DTI, this

Schoodic bus would use the Island Explorer name and paint scheme. Use of propane fuel would required the following: (1) pressurized tanks for winter operation; (2) a heated overnight storage building; and (3) a propane fueling facility. The last two facilities could be provided at the former Navy base on Schoodic Point.

7.2.1.2   Bar Harbor village shuttle

The Jackson Laboratory has expressed an interest in possible year-round shuttle bus service linking the Laboratory with Bar Harbor's downtown residential neighborhoods. It may be possible to design a downtown village shuttle that also accommodates ferry passengers who arrive from Winter Harbor at the Bar Harbor town pier. This arrangement would be much less expensive than operating a separate ferry connector bus.

The ability to serve both markets with one bus will depend on the level of demand from Bar Harbor village residents and from ferry riders. It will also depend on afternoon traffic congestion at the town pier during peak summer months. It may be necessary to utilize separate buses in the afternoon when tourist-related traffic is backed up at the town pier.

This service plan calls for diverting buses from their regular cross-town route to meet arriving ferry commuters in the morning and to deliver departing ferry commuters in the afternoon. It may be possible to utilize a bus from the Island Explorer vehicle fleet from September through mid-June. An additional bus would be needed from mid-June through August, unless the Island Explorer fleet is expanded to accommodate increased summer demand.

As indicated above, a separate ferry shuttle bus may be needed during July, August, and September because of seasonal traffic congestion near the town pier. It will not be acceptable to ask other Jackson Lab commuters to wait for a shuttle vehicle that is delayed by waterfront traffic. It may be possible to schedule a seasonal Island Explorer bus to fill this afternoon gap during July, August, and September. This will require implementation of a plan to expand the current Island Explorer vehicle fleet.

Bar Harbor village shuttle service will involve roughly eight hours of service each weekday. This will result in 2,000 service hours per year, with an anticipated operating cost of $50,000. Additional use of an Island Explorer bus for two hours each weekday during July, August, and September would add roughly 140 service hours at an estimated additional cost of $5,600 per year.

7.2.1.3   Midday Bar Harbor – Acadia National Park bus link

A midday link may be needed to transport ANP staff and Schoodic program participants between the Bar Harbor town pier and ANP headquarters. This transportation link could be provided with an Acadia National Park van. Or it may be possible to adjust Downeast Transportation's year round Bar Harbor bus service to accommodate this need.

DTI currently provides only two-day-a-week midday shuttle service in Bar Harbor. Expanding in-town midday shuttle service to five days a week would involve about five hours per day, or roughly 750 hours per year. This service expansion would cost an estimated $18,750 per year. In addition to the National Park Service, beneficiaries would include Bar Harbor senior citizens and the College of the Atlantic. DTI has submitted a request to MDOT for planning funds to develop strategies for expanding year round bus service on Mount Desert Island.

7.3 Summary of Vehicle Requirements and Cost Projections

Vehicle requirements and operating cost projections are summarized in Table 7-9. Operating cost estimates are based on Downeast Transportation's current unit cost of $25 per hour.

Service Option	Vehicle Needs	Operating cost	Comments
Bus Only Level 1 weekdays only	1 motorcoach @ roughly $250,000 1 medium-duty 28-passenger bus @ $100,000	3,875 annual hours at a cost of $96,875 Optional evening runs could increase the cost to $100,000	Costs would be shared by Acadia National Park, Jackson Laboratory, and fare-paying passengers. The service may be eligible for FTA intercity funding.
Bus Only Level 2 weekdays only	2 motorcoaches @ roughly $250,000 each	5,000 annual hours at a cost of $125,000 Optional evening runs could add between $2,500 and $5,000 per year.	Costs would be shared by Acadia National Park, Jackson Laboratory, and fare-paying passengers. The service may be eligible for FTA intercity funding.
Schoodic bus to meet ferries from Bar Harbor	1 28-passenger Island Explorer bus @ roughly $100,000	2,750 hours of weekday service @ $68,750 per year 364 hours of six-month weekend service @ $9,100 per year	Connecting ferry passengers would not pay an additional fare to ride the bus. ANP transit fees would cover most costs, with possible contributions from towns and local bus riders. The service may be eligible for up to 50% FTA funding.
Bar Harbor village shuttle to meet Winter Harbor ferries	1 28-passenger Island Explorer bus @ roughly $100,000	2,000 weekday hours @ $50,000 per year	Funding would be provided by Jackson Laboratory and the College of the Atlantic. The service may be eligible for up to 50% FTA funding. Passenger fares could be charged to reduce subsidy requirements.

Table 7-8
Summary of Vehicle Requirements and Cost Projections

8 Transportation Alternatives Summary and Selection

The Transportation Alternatives from 1 to 4 represent incrementally more ambitious planning concepts, with a central focus on ferry service. Improvements in bicycling opportunities and bus service are a common thread for all Alternatives and indeed are desirable outcomes whatever the future holds for ferries. Discussion in this chapter therefore is concentrated on ferries and the other modes as they relate to ferry service. More specific findings relating to those modes appear in Chapter 10.

8.1 Alternative 2

Bus only service between Bar Harbor and Winter Harbor would not substantially improve regional transport, particularly since there is already a privately operated service, nor would it effectively address the Park's goal of moving people into and around Schoodic by alternate transport modes. The demand analysis shows that such a service could have limited success with commuters and others on official business between Acadia National Park on MDI and the new activities at the Navy base on Schoodic.

Bus service is not likely, however, to attract substantial numbers of recreational riders, for whom it will not enhance the Park visitor experience. The added time and inconvenience of riding the bus over the same route available to the private automobile would be a serious disincentive, particularly if a good park-and-ride lot is available in Winter Harbor for bicyclists.

8.2 Alternative 3

The ferry economic analysis clearly indicates that fully developed seasonal ferry service could be profitable in all scenarios considered, without any subsidies, when the Navy base redevelopment is complete. The reader should note that the analysis indicated these results on the basis of conservatively high cost assumptions and low fare bases for commuter and recreational passengers.

The ferry service's success would depend in part on other transportation system components put in place under this Alternative. Those components would include bicycle lane improvements in and around the Schoodic parkland, availability of free bicycle transport on the ferry and rented bicycles in Winter Harbor, an automobile park-and-ride facility in central Winter Harbor, local bus service links from both the Bar Harbor and Winter Harbor ferry docks, and bus service between the two towns for the offseason and for unscheduled down time for the ferry.

The analysis of candidate terminals on Schoodic Peninsula showed that the privately operated Winter Harbor Marina dock would be the best choice. In addition to best serving the Park's need for convenience to the Schoodic parkland, it offers the best dock and parking infrastructure, and the least restrictive navigational approach and operating depths. Other docks considered have higher use by local boaters and fishermen in more congested areas and are therefore less viable for scheduled ferry service.

The projected annual ferry operation profit margins favor the selection of single Subchapter T monohull, less than 65' in length (a 50' vessel was the subject of the analyses), over two such boats or a single catamaran. The differences in head time are not great and the speed advantage of the catamaran over the 7 mile route trims only a few minutes from the voyage times. The added capital and operating expenses of two monohulls or a catamaran far outweigh the revenue increment gained by slightly better service frequencies and speeds.

Over 90% of revenues are from recreational users in all cases, because they would constitute most passengers ("demand") and would pay much higher fares (commuter fares are held to $3 one way). Service times and frequencies are much less important for the recreational passenger. The single monohull would, nonetheless, effectively serve commuter needs, as the integrated ferry/bus schedule in Chapter 7 illustrates.

8.3 Alternative 4

The results of the year round ferry service (again with local bus links and backup service, and the noted bicycling mode improvements) analyses are analogous to Alternative #3 as they relate to the efficacy of the particular boats, operational and infrastructure choices, and the character of the patronage and revenue. Offseason service adds considerable capital (only 60% of debt service assumed for seasonal scenarios) and operating expense for little extra income from the fare box. The obvious reason for the latter is that few recreational passengers would use the service and that the fare receipts from commuters would be low. Some service scenarios project losses, i.e., the Low Reuse Concepts with the high capital expense boats. Profit margin in all other cases are considerably less. Additional maintenance and repair, and offseason weather-related cancellations would also affect financial performance.

The results of the finance model taken together with the uncertainties inherent in any economic forecasting argue against year round service, at least initially. Absent capital or operating subsidies, the probability of economic failure would be significantly higher than for seasonal service.

8.4 Selection

Acadia National Park visitation numbers will continue to increase into the foreseeable future, along with the general population growth and the intensification of coastal use. The Schoodic parkland will most likely not be an exception to this trend. The Park must support the development of attractive alternate transportation options for visitors and commuters. Ferry service has obvious visitor experience value to the recreational traveler and practical value to the "Down East" commuter going to work in Bar Harbor; the one, in fact, supports the other.

The economic promise of profitable seasonal ferry operations between Bar Harbor and Winter Harbor points to Alternative 3 as the best choice at this time. A single monohull service would provide adequate frequency and speed for the commuter and could be the centerpiece of a very attractive day trip package (including circle bus service and bicycling opportunities in Schoodic) for recreational passengers. The high profit margins for these scenarios indicate low financial risk for the operator, for whom the option of a second boat and/or year round service would be available after the service's start-up period.

The bus service schedules presented in Chapter 7 show the efficacy of providing local inter-modal service links at both ferry terminals, as well as the Bar Harbor/Winter Harbor service needed for off-season and other ferry service interruptions. The bicycling opportunities arising from provision of bicycle lanes around Schoodic, conveniently located park-and-ride lots, and bicycle rentals are an integral part of Alternative 3 and should be a goal of the Park for the future as well.

Whichever the Park Service chooses as its preferred alternative, environmental review per the requirements of the National Environmental Policy Act (NEPA) will be required before proceeding to further analysis and implementation activities.

9 Schoodic Peninsula Roadway Impacts and Enhancements

Vehicular traffic in the Schoodic area is projected to increase at a rate of slightly more than 1% a year over the next 15 years on the major routes and slightly less for local roads, without accounting for additional traffic generated by Navy base reuse activities. The base generated about 350 vehicle trips daily when in full use, up through the mid-1990s. These traffic volumes were fairly constant in those years but had decreased by at least 50% by the year 2000 due to the gradual reductions of its work force.

The roadway impacts for the High and Low Reuse Concepts and Transportation Alternatives are measured by two traffic metrics: 1) average daily traffic (ADT) on the roadways; and 2) volume to capacity (V/C) ratio. Both metrics are the basis of comparison to base line traffic in the year 2000. The traffic analysis for the three active Transportation Alternatives distinguishes commuter and recreational trips by for the four major roadway segments, which are SR 186 between Winter Harbor and Birch Harbor, Moore Rd in Winter Harbor, Schoodic Point Road, and Wonsqueak Rd in Gouldsboro.

Table 9-1 summarizes the roadway traffic characterization and is the basis of discussion in the following subsections. The discussion of each alternative focuses on the ADT value changes relative to the 2000 baseline values. Current ADTs are 2000 on SR186 and from 700 to 800 in and directly adjacent to the Schoodic parkland. Table 9-1 should be examined for details.

9.1 Transportation Alternative 1

The No Action alternative would result in the highest roadway traffic volumes in both 2005 and 2015 for all scenarios, and the Concept 3 "High Reuse" scenario would be the worst case. The roadways would be unchanged in this Alternative. Commuters destined to the base would originate throughout Schoodic Peninsula and the surrounding communities. Work trips to the base would account for only about 20% of all vehicle trips using the roadway; this value varies only slightly for the different Reuse Concepts because the proportion of work trips is so low relative to total trips. Work trips peak in the early morning and late afternoon commuting hours. Outside of these peaks, commuters to the base would not significantly contribute to traffic on any of the local roadways.

Most recreational trips would be via USR 1, SR 186, and Moore Road, leading to the base or the Schoodic Point visitor area, where more then 88% of all recreational trips would be destined. Vehicular traffic increases in all scenarios are mitigated because of the initial removal of the traffic associated with the baseline use of the base, approximately 300 vehicles daily.

Alternative		Rte 186, E. of Moore Rd				Moore Rd, outside Park				Schoodic Point Rd				Wonsqueak Rd, outside			
		Cap.	ADT	ADT/12	V/C	Cap.	ADT	ADT/12	V/C	Cap.	ADT	ADT/12	V/C	Cap.	ADT	ADT/12	V/C
Base Year																	
	Year 2000	2,000	2,000	167	0.08	1,800	800	67	0.04	900	720	60	0.07	1,800	800	67	0.04
Alternative 1																	
	Year 2005																
No	Low	2,000	2,050	171	0.09	1,800	780	65	0.04	900	700	58	0.06	1,800	780	65	0.04
	High	2,000	2,250	188	0.09	1,800	800	67	0.04	900	720	60	0.07	1,800	800	67	0.04
	Year 2015																
Action	Low	2,000	2,170	181	0.09	1,800	820	68	0.04	900	740	62	0.07	1,800	820	68	0.04
	High	2,000	2,400	200	0.1	1,800	970	81	0.04	900	880	73	0.08	1,800	970	81	0.04
Alternative 2																	
	Year 2005																
Bus	Low	2,000	2,030	169	0.08	900	760	63	0.07	900	680	57	0.06	900	760	63	0.07
	High	2,000	2,210	184	0.09	900	780	65	0.07	900	700	58	0.06	900	780	65	0.07
Service	Year 2015																
	Low	2,000	2,150	179	0.09	900	800	67	0.07	900	720	60	0.07	900	800	67	0.07
Only	High	2,000	2,360	197	0.1	900	950	79	0.09	900	860	72	0.08	900	950	79	0.09
Alternative 3																	
	Year 2005																
Seasonal	Low	2,000	2,000	167	0.08	900	730	61	0.07	900	660	55	0.06	900	730	61	0.07
	High	2,000	2,180	182	0.09	900	760	63	0.07	900	670	56	0.06	900	760	63	0.07
	Year 2015																
Ferry	Low	2,000	2,120	177	0.09	900	770	64	0.07	900	700	58	0.06	900	770	64	0.07
	High	2,000	2,320	193	0.1	900	920	77	0.09	900	830	69	0.08	900	920	77	0.09
Alternative 4																	
	Year 2005																
Year	Low	2,000	1,990	166	0.08	900	720	60	0.07	900	650	54	0.06	900	720	60	0.07
	High	2,000	2,170	181	0.09	900	750	63	0.07	900	660	55	0.06	900	750	63	0.07
Round	Year 2015																
	Low	2,000	2,110	176	0.09	900	760	63	0.07	900	680	57	0.06	900	760	63	0.07
Ferry	High	2,000	2,310	193	0.1	900	900	75	0.08	900	810	68	0.08	900	900	75	0.08

NOTES:
Cap. = Daily roadway capacity
ADT = Average Daily Traffic
ADT/12 = Average hourly distribution of total daily traffic, over 12 hours only
V/C = Roadway volume / Capacity

Table 9-1
Schoodic Area Vehicular Traffic

9.1.1 Impacts

Summarized results of the traffic analysis follow:

- SR 186 would handle more traffic in all reuse scenarios relative to the baseline. The ADTs change in the range of +50 – +400, the lowest value corresponding to the Low Reuse, 2005 scenario and the highest to the High Reuse, 2015 scenario. The daily V/C ratio is about 0.08 for the base year. In none of the scenarios for 2005 and 2015 does this value exceed 0.10, which represents a very modest increase over current levels.

- Moore Road and Wonsqueak Road have higher capacities than the roads inside the park due to their widths, shoulders, and access. The ADTs change in the range of -20 - +170, these extreme values corresponding to the same scenarios . The V/C stays fairly constant throughout all of the scenarios.

- The ADT values for the segments of Moore Road and Wonsqueak Road inside the Park are the same as those calculated for those roads outside the Park. Their traffic capacity is reduced, however, resulting in slightly higher V/C ratios (increasing from 0.06to– 0.07). Bicycles and vehicles parking on the side of the road could cause more congestion and safety concerns.

- The roadway to Schoodic Point will see a slight reduction in the Low 2005 scenario but will increase to current levels in the High 2005 scenario. The Low 2015 scenario sees an increase of 40 vehicles over current conditions but is expected to increase by 160 in the High 2015 scenario. There is the potential that people could use the base as a parking area unless it is restricted to authorized vehicles.
- The parking lots inside the park will fill to capacity more frequently, especially in the High Reuse scenarios, due mainly to increased volume of recreational trips.
- The reader should note that, in all scenarios, the V/C ratios reported are daily average numbers which would of course include significantly higher peaks because of seasonal variations (i.e., summer) and daily variations (commuter hours and midday recreational peak hours). The daily averages are in any case a good measure of relative volume and capacity.

9.1.2 Enhancements

There are no roadway enhancements for the no action Transportation Alternative.

9.2 Transportation Alternative 2

A year bus service linking Bar Harbor and the Schoodic Peninsula would serve both commuters and recreational users with seven daily trips on USR 1 and SR 3 between Bar Harbor & Schoodic averaging 1 hour and 25 minutes one way. The projected demand during the summer season would be equally divided between commuters and recreational trips, while during the off-season, commuters would be the dominant element. The service would be integrated with the Downeast Service and the Island Explorer, with fares similar to others in their schedule.

9.2.1 Impacts

The bus only Alternative would remove between 20 vehicles daily (2005, Low Reuse, Concept 1) and 40 vehicles daily (2015, High Reuse, Concept 3) from SR 186 east of Moore Road. The buses will need pick-up and drop-off areas inside and outside the Navy base. This could decrease traffic flow during pick-up and drop-off situations, but, given the limited number of trips and stops, this should not be a problem along this roadway. The resulting V/C ratios are in the range of 0.08 to 0.10, slightly lower than those for Alternative 3.

Moore Road and Wonsqueak Road would see reduction of about 20 vehicles daily for all Reuse Concepts in 2005 and 2015. Infrequent service and long travel time compared to personal vehicles will not entice recreational passengers, most of whom would choose to drive. The V/C would increase significantly from the base year 2000 in all of the alternatives, conceptual plans, and years, because of the presumed capacity reduction along the Park roads for bicycle lanes. This would limit vehicle use to one lane and devote the second lane to bicycle use and shoulder parking. Even with an increase from 0.04 to 0.09, the impact for the driver on the road would not be significant except during peak days of the summer months.

Schoodic Point Road would have a similar traffic reduction. The V/C ratios show little change, between a reduction of 0.01 to an increase of 0.01 along this stretch of roadway. Traffic turning into the base, especially left hand turns by east-bound cars, could cause occasional traffic delays. This two way roadway segment is very narrow and could cause safety problems if not widened to include a bike lane. Bus service here could occasionally cause minor traffic problems in the visitor parking area during stops for boardings and alightings but this should be only be a problem during peak times.

9.2.2 Enhancements

Several enhancements to the local roadways and supporting activities should be considered to help the bus alternative function as smoothly as possible.

- SR 186 needs of maintenance and expansion in several areas. The maintenance consists of repairing the pavement and re-striping the shoulder lanes and the bike lanes and widening would allow for the inclusion of a bicycle lane and for turning lanes at the major intersections. This stretch of roadway should be limited access and allow for stops only where it meets East Schoodic Road and Moore Road.
- Enhancements to Moore Road and Wonsqueak Road, both inside and outside the park, need consideration. The options inside the park are limited by the IDS-HPGTCL. The roads should continue to be one-way from Frazier Point to Schoodic Point Rd then North to Birch Harbor. This would allow for the least amount of impact to the roadway and still permit a bike lane with shoulder to be included. Stops should be limited to the following locations:
  - ➢ Frazier Point
  - ➢ The Base
  - ➢ Schoodic Point
  - ➢ Blueberry Hill
  - ➢ Park Exit near Wonsqueak Harbor

The stops should be well marked and include the schedule of operations. They should also be in locations that allow for vehicles and bicycles to pass without safety concerns.

- Schoodic Point Road needs widening to allow for a shoulder with a bike lane to be added from the loop road down to the parking area on Schoodic Point. A right hand turning lane on southbound side of Schoodic Point Rd. into the Navy base also should be included. To limit congestion caused by left hand turns into the Navy base from vehicles leaving Schoodic Point, a ban on left hand turns should be considered during peak summer months. To minimize parking problems, excess visitor parking for Schoodic Point should be allowed on the base during peak summer months. To enhance bicycle use all buses should be equipped with bicycle racks.

9.3 Transportation Alternative 3

Commuter and recreational trip making patterns change in the study area because of diversions from the automotive mode to ferry and bus, and the use of park-and ride lots, particularly between Sorrento and Bar Harbor. Commuter trips originating east of

Schoodic Peninsula to use the ferry would be diverted from USR 1 to SR 186 as they transit to the park-and-ride lot at the Winter Harbor marina dock, increasing traffic slightly on SR 186 from USR 1 to Birch Harbor to Winter Harbor. Recreational trips would be reduced along SR 186, Moore Road and Wonsqueak Road due to diversions to bus service. Traffic would increase along Main Street in Winter Harbor due to bus traffic and the use of the Winter Harbor Town Center Park-and-Ride Lot.

9.3.1 Impacts

Summarized results of the traffic analysis follow:

- SR 186 would handle more traffic in all reuse scenarios relative to the baseline. The ADT changes relative to the baseline range from zero for the Low Reuse, 2005 scenario to +320 for the High Reuse 2015 scenario. When compared to Alternative 1, these are all decreases in vehicular traffic. Recreational vehicle trips decrease while commuter vehicle trips going to the Winter Harbor dock cause an increase. The V/C ratios are very close to those for Alternative 1.
- Both Moore and Wonsqueak Roads would see ADT reductions between 30 and 70 vehicles daily relative to the base year for all except the High Reuse 2015 scenario, for which ADT would increase by 120. The V/C ratios would not differ significantly from the base year.
- Moore and Wonsqueak Roads inside the park would see similar levels of traffic as outside the park, but the V/C ratios could increase significantly if one of the two lanes of the one-way loop is used as a bike lane. This would be exacerbated by a higher percentages of recreational trips than in the base year, associated with which are more frequent stops, slower speeds, and parking at scenic spots.
- Schoodic Point Road is the main access to the base and is frequented by almost 90% of all of the recreational trips to Schoodic Peninsula. This area has limited parking and experiences parking shortages during the peak summer months. The roadway entering the parking lot area is narrow with little to no shoulder for bicyclist. This roadway will have V/C ratios between 0.06 and 0.08.

9.3.2 Enhancements

There are several potential enhancements to the roadway that can improve travel or reduce traffic, categorized as roadway improvements and transportation systems management (TSM). Roadway improvements enhance traffic capacity and flow through better performance of maintenance or expansion of the roadway itself. TSM measures maximize the effectiveness of the system through operational, communications, and other "soft" techniques. These might include variable message signs (VMS) with status of parking lots, congestion alerts, and alternate route suggestions. It is also important to maintain a current and accurate database on park use and traffic through the use of traffic counters on the roadways and at the visitor areas.

Specific candidate enhancements for the consideration of roadway managers are the following:

- SR 186 is in need of maintenance and expansion. Maintenance needs include pavement repair and lane re-striping (Schoodic Byway Committee). Roadway expansion would accommodate bicycle lanes on the shoulders and turning lanes at the major intersections. While AASHTO specifies separate shoulders and breakdown lanes in association with bicycle lanes, the focus of these guidelines is on high traffic volume areas; that requirement is not necessary or feasible in this area. TSM measures would include improved traditional signage and/or VMS.

- Candidate enhancements to Moore Road and Wonsqueak Road outside the Park include paving of the shoulders and widening in selected locations to provide for bike lanes on both sides. Wonsqueak Road has a very narrow shoulder whose expansion may require easements or land acquisitions for a ROW.
- Enhancements to Moore Road and Wonsqueak Road inside the Park are limited by the IDS-HPGTCL. The recommendation herein is that they should continue to be one-way from Frazer Point down to Schoodic Point then back to Birch Harbor. This approach would cause the least impact to the roadway while allowing for a bicycle lane. Any widening considered should be to the left (landward) side of the road where degradation of the area's natural beauty is minimized; removal of copingstones must in all cases be minimized. The cost of this kind of work averages between $100,000 to $200,000 per mile depending on the project's particulars, and would probably suffice for these suggested improvements, including a bicycle path on the right most lane. Parking should be restricted to the visitor parking areas so that "casual" roadside parking does not restrict bicycle movement and degrade safety. Traffic counters should be maintained at the Schoodic parkland's entry and exit points.
- The spur road to Schoodic Point and the Navy base would require expansion and TSM measures to mitigate increased traffic volumes. The roadway should be widened to accommodate a bicycle lane into the parking area. The roadway should be striped or marked to identify that pedestrians and bicyclists have the right of way. Allowing for an overflow lot to be located on the base property would expand parking. A camera showing traffic delays in the parking area would allow Park staff to manually or electronically update the VMS in Winter Harbor. A traffic counter should be installed somewhere on Schoodic Point Road to track use of the parking lot.

9.4 Transportation Alternative 4

Transportation Alternative 4 differs from Alternative 3 only in that it would continue ferry service year round, i.e., into the offseason. The impacts and enhancements are similar to Alternative 3; there may, however, be lesser, minor variations in the ADT and the V/C's during the offseason relative to the "no action" Transportation Alternative. Commuter trips using the ferry year round would cause a small reduction in vehicle trips on USR 1, but cause a corresponding increase along SR 186. The roadways into and out of the park would see little if any change in ADT relative to Alternative 3. The large majority of recreational vehicular trips occur during the seasonal time period (May - October), and the seasonal traffic would be identical to that for Alternative 3.

9.4.1 Impacts

The impacts would be similar to Alternative 3.

9.4.2 Enhancements

The recommended enhancements would be the same Alternative 3.

9.5 Summary

The key roadway analysis quantifies the effect of the active Transportation Alternatives (2, 3, and 4) on the roadways relative to the Alternative 1, the no action approach. The brief analysis which follows undertakes a comparison of each scenario (i.e., high/low reuse concept, year) for the active alternatives relative to the same scenario for Alternative 1. The premise is that some reuse of the Navy base will occur and the years 2005 and 2015 will come to pass, regardless of action taken to develop alternative transportation options. The results illuminate the true benefits of the active alternatives in lower traffic volumes (ADTs) on the roads. The ADT values understate the effectiveness of the active alternatives at times of peak demand and at system chokepoints, particularly parking lots. The results appear in Table 9-2.

Table 9-2 shows clearly that the incrementally more aggressive transportation system development represented by Alternatives 2, 3, and 4 result in progressively higher benefits in terms of removing automobiles from the Schoodic area roads. The effect is also greater in the year 2015 because of the higher levels of both recreational and commuter travel anticipated.

All of the Alternatives should include the roadway transportation system management initiatives advanced herein, including new signage (e.g., variable message boards) and monitoring of traffic for both real time management and accurate long term data collection.

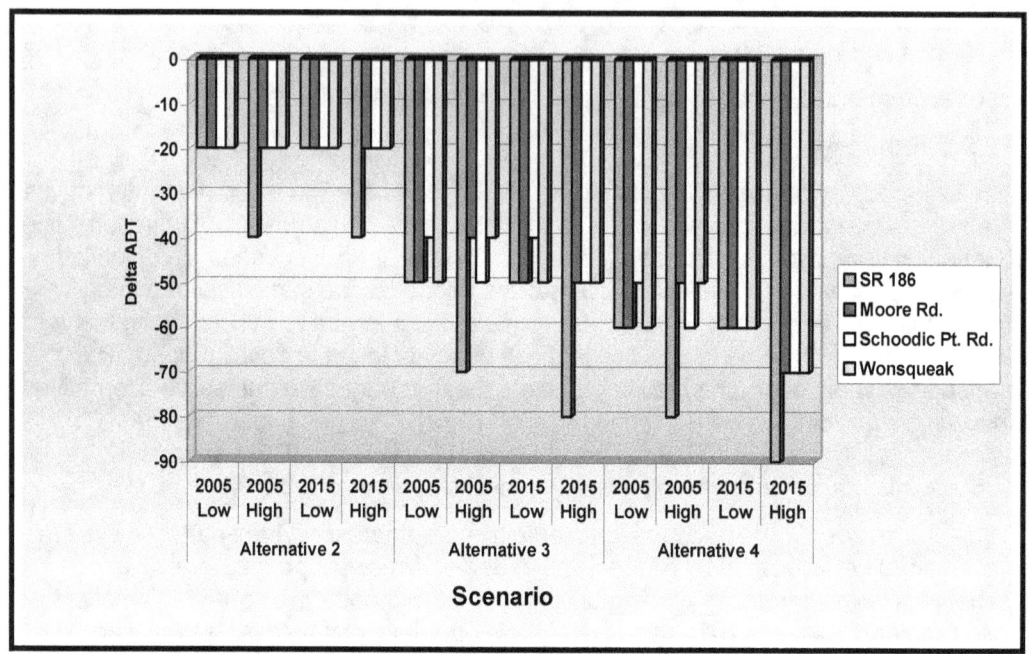

Note: "Delta ADT" denotes the change in average daily traffic.

Figure 9-1
Roadway Traffic:
Effect of Active Alternatives Relative to "No Action" Alternative

10 Findings and Recommendations

The Park Service faces a dilemma in planning for the future of the Schoodic Peninsula parkland. The local needs of Down East communities affected by the Navy base closure dictate its reuse in a way that sustains, in a roughly similar way, the economic and demographic character of the area. The Park's goal of preserving the quiet, unspoiled nature of the Schoodic parkland requires an effort to mitigate the increasing levels of automobile traffic which now carry nearly all visitors into the area. This report has shown that Transportation Alternatives combining new ferry service from Mount Desert Island to Schoodic Peninsula with enhanced bus and bicycling opportunities are technically and economically feasible and could carry significant numbers of trip-to-work and recreational travelers. It is possible and perhaps probable that the private sector will see the opportunity and move to develop such a service, perhaps as the initial stage of a future expanded regional service taking on some of the elements embodied in the State of Maine's transportation strategy.

The Park Service must face the possibility that such transportation services will have the conflicting effects of mitigating automobile traffic and inducing increased demand for travel, particularly for recreational users. Travel to Acadia National Park, including Schoodic Peninsula, is likely to increase over the period considered for this study, and the question will be whether the effect of induced demand outweighs the benefit of reduced automobile traffic. The estimates for recreational patronage do not indicate that total visitation to Schoodic would rise dramatically over the current level of 11% of total Acadia visitors. The development of future alternative transportation services is a strong possibility in any event and the Park Service should take an active role in shaping its role.

The Park Service appears to have limited leverage in the process of future ferry service development, since no concessions involving Park land for dock and terminal facilities would be necessary. The Park can, however, exert influence through their role in the development of the necessary inter-modal transportation links (i.e., buses), cooperative arrangements with the ferry operator in the enhancement of the visitor experience (e.g., rangers onboard for interpretive voyages, publicity for the service), and the possibility of direct or indirect subsidies. The prospect of a successful ferry service to Schoodic Peninsula is tantalizing as the results of this study show; Acadia National Park will need to be an actively involved partner in order to achieve the desired balance of attractive Transportation Alternative and the measured pace of growth in the future for Schoodic Peninsula.

10.1 Selection of Transportation Alternative

The Park must support the development of attractive alternate transportation options for visitors and commuters. Ferry service provides both visitor experience value to the recreational traveler and practical value to the "Down East" commuter going to work in Bar Harbor. These markets support each other.

The promise of profitable seasonal ferry operations between Bar Harbor and Winter Harbor points to Alternative 3 as the best choice at this time. A single monohull service would provide adequate frequency and speed for the commuter and would be the centerpiece of a very attractive Schoodic day trip package (with bus and bicycling opportunities) for recreational passengers. The high profit margins for the seasonal scenarios indicate low financial risk for the operator, for whom the option of a second boat and/or year round service would be available once the service is on firm footing.

Schoodic-to-MDI bus service would provide needed coverage for the off-season and other ferry service interruptions. Local bus service links at both ferry terminals would perform both transit and excursion duties at both ends. The bicycling opportunities arising from provision of bicycle lanes around Schoodic, conveniently located park-and-ride lots, and bicycle rentals are an integral part of Alternative 3 and should be a goal of the Park for the future as well.

10.2   Ferry Services

The ferry economic analysis indicates that fully developed seasonal service could be profitable in all scenarios considered, without any subsidies, when the Navy base redevelopment is complete, and is based on a number of conservatively high cost assumptions and low fare bases for commuter and recreational passengers.

The projected annual ferry operation profit margins favor the selection of single Subchapter T monohull, less than 65' in length (a 50' vessel was the subject of one set of analyses), over two such boats or a single catamaran. The differences in head time are not great and the speed advantage of the catamaran over the 7 mile route trims only a few minutes from the voyage times. Nonetheless, the single monohull would certainly serve commuter needs effectively, as the integrated ferry/bus schedule in Chapter 7 illustrates. The added capital and operating expenses of two monohulls or a catamaran far outweigh the revenue increment gained by slightly better service frequencies and speeds. The net annual profit/loss for all scenarios appears in Figure 10-1, repeated from Chapter 5.

Over 90% of projected revenues are from recreational users in all cases, because they would constitute most passengers ("demand") and would pay much higher fares (commuter fares are held to $3 one way). Service times and frequencies are much less important for the recreational passenger. Round trip patronage numbers for the 2005 seasonal scenarios range from 23,660 to 47,138 recreational passengers and from 3,770 to 5,200 commuters. In the 2015 scenarios, the numbers of recreational passengers rise between 18% and 22% and commuters between 22% and 27%, relative to 2005.

The analysis of candidate terminals on Schoodic Peninsula showed that the privately operated Winter Harbor Marina dock would be the best choice. In addition to best serving the Park's need for convenience to the Schoodic parkland, it offers the best dock and parking infrastructure, and the least restrictive navigational approach and operating depths. Other docks examined had much higher use by local boaters and fishermen in more congested areas. The superiority of the Winter Harbor Marina dock more than compensates for the relative disadvantages of the length and exposed waters of its route relative to the South Gouldsboro route.

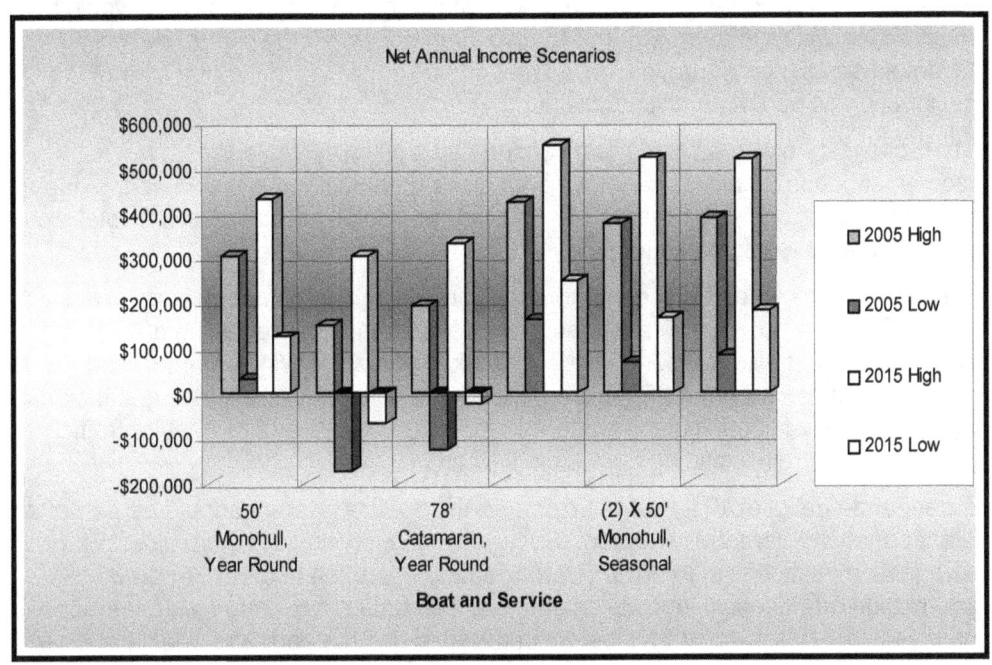

Figure 10-1
Net Annual Ferry Service Finances

10.3   Bicycle Transport Enhancements

The consideration of bicycle transport enhancements went forward with the National Scenic Byway designation for most of the affected roads and the proposed designation of the Schoodic parkland as a National Resource District in mind. Most suggested improvements to roads in the park come forward with the premise that the roads' configuration cannot be changed. This report adopts a number of bicycle lane improvements suggested in the National Scenic Byway proposal for roads outside the Park.

Bicycle usage demand arising from the implementation of new transportation options is high. Analysis of Transportation Alternative 3 yielded the following results: year 2005, from 35,248 to 61,207; year 2015, from 39,954 to 73,939. The projected numbers of total bicyclists for Alternative 2 are identical, including 5% to 6% who would ride the bus to Schoodic. The results for Alternative 4 were virtually the same since so few would choose to ride bicycles in the winter months.

The goal of providing a safe bicycle route through the Schoodic parkland, one that adheres to AASHTO guidelines, is best attained by retaining the one-way loop configuration from Frazer Point to the Park exit at Birch Harbor and reassigning the existing lanes as follows: one lane for vehicular traffic, and the seaward lane for 5' wide bicycle lane and a 5' extended shoulder. Striping, signage, and pavement markings are important elements of the conversion that would have minimal impact on the roadway. Some restriction of traffic flow would occur at peak periods, but the effect would be mitigated by promoting the use of the park-and-ride lots, ferries, and buses and reducing automobile traffic. Otherwise, expansion of the roadway's width would be required for a bicycle path, whether for two lane, one-way or two lane, two-way automobile traffic configuration. The latter choice depends on the outcome of the road's designation as part of an historic district.

The Schoodic Point spur road must continue as a two way vehicular way. The recommendation for bicycle lanes on both sides means that this would be the one area requiring road surface expansion. This would be a small proportion of the total length of roads in the Schoodic parkland.

Outside the park land, the specifics of the bicycle lane improvements suggested in the Scenic Byway proposal are reiterated here: paved shoulders replacing gravel on both sides of the Schoodic Road in Gouldsboro, Moore Road in Winter Harbor, and SR 186 between Winter Harbor and Birch Harbor, along with bicycle lane striping and pavement signs. This need is particularly acute along SR 186 because of its heavier traffic, higher speeds, and terrain including numerous hills and curves.

A park-and-ride lot at Misty Harbor Apartments in Winter Harbor should be part of any Transportation Alternative adopted. Such a conversion would require bicycle racks, and a variable message sign in Winter Harbor on the approach to Main Street with information on Schoodic loop road traffic and the status of parking inside the Schoodic parkland. Motorists would thus be encouraged to use the park-and-ride lot at peak times. option of using a park-and-ride lot in central Winter Harbor and transferring to loop bus service or bicycles. Bicycle amenities are also recommended at the ferry dock for Alternatives 3 and 4.

10.4   Bus Service

Chapter 7 includes detailed schedule proposals for Bar Harbor to Winter Harbor service and local loop services in each town. These are designed to met the needs of many ridership markets, most particularly residents and users of the Navy base in its future makeup. The services' variations meet the different intents of the four Transportation Alternatives, namely no ferry service and seasonal and year round services between Bar Harbor and Winter Harbor. In the latter cases, an integrated bus and ferry schedule demonstrates how a rider from the Schoodic area or further east would make all the necessary mode shifts to commute to Jackson Laboratory in Bar Harbor and back.

"Level One" service would provide limited commuter and midday links between the Schoodic Peninsula and Bar Harbor with one 35 or 40 passenger bus and would suffice for Alternative 2 bus only service or Alternative 3 offseason service. "Level Two" service addresses the same Alternatives with two such buses and more frequent runs, aimed at a wider variety of people conducting business at or with new activities at the Navy base.

The local bus links are designed for minimal mode change times at the ferry docks on either end. These would serve both commuter and recreational riders with a single 28 passenger bus.

The Level One service would cost approximately $97,000 per year to operate 3,875 hours; the figures for Level Two service are $125,000 and 5,000 hours per year. The annual cost of the Schoodic Peninsula link service would be $69,000 for weekday service and an additional $9,000 for weekends. The Bar Harbor shuttle service would cost $50,000 per year for weekday service.

10.5   Roadway Impacts and Enhancements

Traffic on the Schoodic roads would increase steadily in the coming years due to population and Park visitation growth. These increases are mitigated by all the active Transportation Alternatives as measured by Average Daily Traffic (ADT). Volume to Capacity ratios do not change dramatically on the affected roads since long time scale averages are involved. The beneficial effect of transportation system enhancements in the form of new ferry and bus services would be concentrated at times of peak demand and at system chokepoints, particularly parking lots.

The key measure is the difference in ADT values in the future between the active Transportation Alternatives (2, 3, and 4) and Alternative 1, the no action approach. Table 9-2, repeated here as 10-2, shows those values for all scenarios (i.e., high/low reuse concept, year) for the active alternatives relative to Alternative 1. The benefits of the active Transportation Alternatives are clear, and increase with the incrementally more aggressive transportation system development approaches represented by Alternatives 2, 3, and 4. The effect is also greater in the year 2015 because of the higher levels of both recreational and commuter travel anticipated.

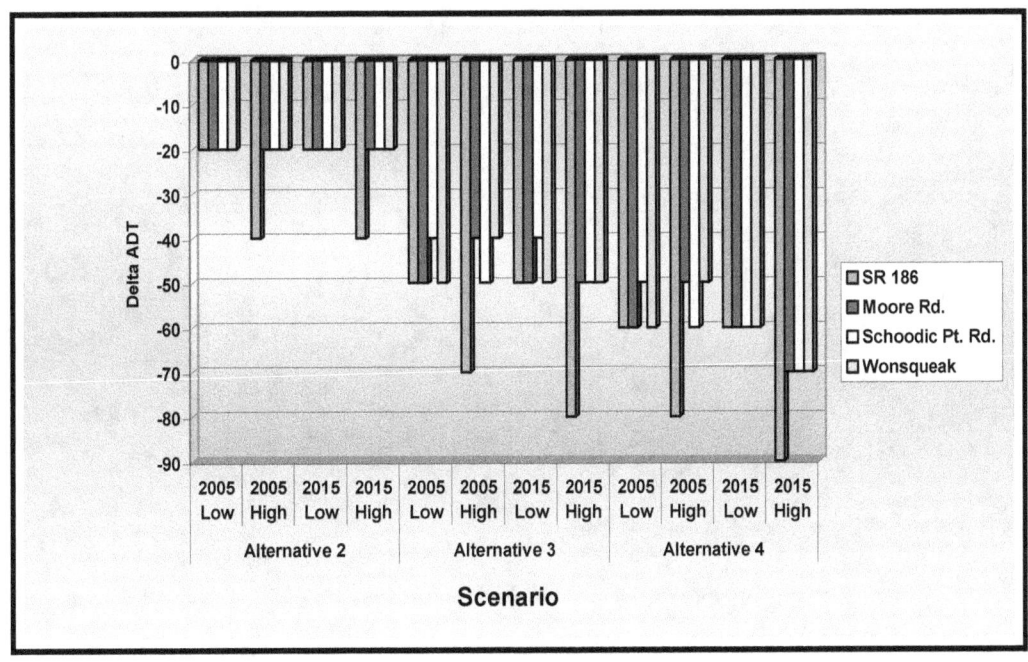

Figure 10-2
Change in Average Daily Traffic:
Effect of Active Alternatives Relative to "No Action" Alternative

REFERENCES

Acadia National Park, General Management Plan, 1994.

American Association of State Highway Transportation Officials (AASHTO)

AASHTO "Guide for the Development of Bicycle Facilities", 1998.

Bicycle Pedestrian Subcommittee for the Region Two Transportation Advisory Committee, Draft Report, September, 2000.

Bustins Island Village Corporation, 2001 Annual Meeting Warrant.

Colgan, Charles, Population Forecasts prepared from Policy Insight Models, University of Southern Maine Website, February 2000.

Federal Highway Administration "Implementing Bicycle Improvements at the Local Level", Publication #FHWA-98-105, 1998.

Hancock County Planning Commission "Schoodic Bar Harbor Feasibility Study", 1996.

Hancock County Planning Commission "Schoodic Bar Harbor Ferry Feasibility Study", October, 1998.

Hancock County Planning Commission Website, 2001.

Institute of Transportation Engineers "Transportation Planning Handbook", 1993 edition.

Littlejohn, Margaret "Summer of 1998 Visitor Study",1999.

Maine State DOT "Strategic Passenger Transportation Plan", Spring 1999.

Schoodic Scenic Byway Corridor Management Committee "Project Summary 2002, FHWA National Scenic Byways Program Grant Application", May 2001.

Town of Gouldsboro, Comprehensive Growth Plan, 1993.

Town of Winter Harbor, Comprehensive Growth Plan, 1994.

Volpe National Transportation Systems Center "High Speed Vessels to Market: Comparative Case Studies in the Passenger Trade", prepared for the Office of Naval Research, September, 2001.

Volpe National Transportation Systems Center "The National Ferry Database", prepared for the Federal Highway Administration, December 2000.

APPENDIX A

Draft Reuse Alternatives

DRAFT Alternative Reuse Concepts
Schoodic Peninsula General Management Plan Amendment
Acadia National Park • Maine

Please note that all concepts are intended to meet stated goals and principles for this plan and that environmental impacts of concepts will be analyzed and reviewed by the public before a course of action is decided.

Concept 1

This concept represents the most site restoration of all the alternatives while supporting a modest learning center. Only the historic structures and facilities necessary for park support and the learning center would remain. Under this concept, visitors would continue to enjoy an uncrowded park experience. Recreational facilities would not expand, but there would be increased interpretive and educational opportunities.

This allows for the learning center to be located in Buildings 1 (Rockefeller) and 84 (dormitory), which would include a laboratory, classrooms, offices, and accommodations for up to 190 students and 5 to 10 researchers. Building 105 (galley) would remain for food service. A small exhibit area and visitor contact station would be located on the first floor of Building 1, which would include a book sales operation and information about the site's history.

The network of hiking trails connecting the base to the National Park lands around the perimeter of Big Moose Island would be opened to the public.

Park operations would be located in Building 216 (public works), which would include offices, storage, garages, and meeting rooms. NPS staff at Schoodic would include permanent maintenance, protection, administrative, and interpretive positions, in addition to those needed to operate the learning center programs.

The water tower would be removed and a new and smaller potable water system would be installed. The existing wastewater treatment facility would be scaled back to handle decreased demand.

The system of roads, paths, parking lots, and open space would be reconfigured to create a more efficient and pleasant campus environment.

The remaining portions of the disturbed site, once cleared of structures, would be restored to the appropriate native plant communities. About 40 acres of disturbed landscape would be restored.

Accommodations would be available for up to 200 people in dormitories and apartments. The learning center may have as many as 200 program users on site on a peak day. The Schoodic unit of the park would experience a moderate increase in visitor day use but have much less overnight use than it does today.

Building Use Summary:

Bldg. 1:   Research facilities, including laboratory and library; apartment housing for researchers and/or park staff; learning center administration office; visitor contact station with exhibits and book sales

Bldg. 2:   Generator house

Bldg. 9:   Gatehouse/visitor contact station

Bldg. 45:   Generator house

Bldg. 84:   190 beds for students, classroom/meeting space

Bldg. 105:   Food service with full-service kitchen and cafeteria

Bldg. 183:   Wastewater treatment facility

Bldg. 216:   Park operations with offices, workshop, garages, storage, and meeting room

Bldg. 225:   Sand/salt storage

Bldg. 228:   Potable water treatment facility

Concept 2

This concept focuses on research and education facilities for the proposed learning center at Acadia, which will promote science and scholarship while informing and educating students of all ages about important natural and cultural conservation issues and the application of research results. It will offer a variety of programs for people of all ages in the fields of natural and cultural history, conservation, science, music, and art. Programs might include, for example, scientific research, environmental education, artists-in-residence, life-long learning, and university extensions. Facilities would include housing, food service, classrooms, and laboratory space. The learning center would operate under a new organization supported by the National Park Service and other partnership organizations, and would use the facilities at Schoodic as a base of operations for research and educational activities consistent with the mission of Acadia National Park.

Learning center programs would be clustered in the center of the current Navy base. Programs would be offered in Building 39 (commissary), where 2 classrooms or laboratories would be located along with an outdoor classroom, and a small office for the learning center. Building 1 (Rockefeller) would provide exhibit space, a small visitor center, and offices for the learning center and its partnership organizations. Building 105 (galley) would provide food service with its full-service kitchen and cafeteria. Other program space would be available in Building 164 (child development center) which would house a small theater and in Building 143 (Schooner Club) which has a kitchen, a classroom and 2 dining or meeting rooms with a capacity of 50 people each. The Navy's history at Schoodic and Mount Desert Island would be interpreted in the original portion of Building 3, which would be restored to its former appearance. Other learning center facilities would be housed in the remaining portions of the building, now the base chapel, including offices and 3 classrooms or laboratories.

The learning center could provide housing for 15-20 researchers and up to 100 students. Students would be housed in Building 84 (dormitory), or in the onsite campground in the summer months. Researchers and park staff would be accommodated in the Schoodic Shores housing complex, from which 16 apartments and garages would be removed, for a remaining 16 two-bedroom apartments. The campground and picnic pavilion would remain for learning center use, and a group camping area would be constructed where the ball field is now situated.

The system of roads, paths, parking lots, and open space would be reconfigured to create a more efficient and pleasant campus environment.

Park operations would be located in Building 216 (public works), and would include offices, storage, garages, and a meeting room. Archival collections would be stored and maintained in Building 162, now a bowling alley. The number of NPS personnel at Schoodic would depend upon the operational and programmatic needs of the learning center, and would include full-time, permanent maintenance, protection, administrative, and interpretive positions. The current wastewater treatment facility and potable water system, including the water tower, would remain.

The remaining portions of the disturbed site, once cleared of structures, would be restored to the appropriate native plant communities. About 16 acres of disturbed landscape would be restored.

Accommodations would be available for up to 300 people in campsites, apartments, and dormitories. The learning center might have as many as 500 program users on site on a peak day.

The Schoodic unit of the park would experience a moderate increase in visitor day use, but it would have less overnight use than it does today.

Building Use Summary:

Bldg. 1:	Visitor center, exhibits, book sales, offices
Bldg. 2:	Generator house
Bldg. 3:	Navy interpretive exhibits, offices, and 3 classrooms/laboratories
Bldg. 9:	Gatehouse/visitor contact station
Bldg. 39:	2 classrooms/laboratories, outdoor classroom
Bldg. 45:	Generator house
Bldg. 84:	190 beds for students
Bldg. 105:	Food service with full-service kitchen and cafeteria
Bldg. 139:	Picnic pavilion to serve 15-site campground and group camping area
Bldg. 141:	Water tower
Bldg. 143:	1 classroom, kitchen, 2 meeting rooms
Bldg. 162:	Park archives
Bldg. 164:	Theater
Bldg. 183:	Wastewater treatment facility
Bldgs. 184, 185, 190, 191:	Schoodic Shores 16 townhouses for researchers and employees
Bldg. 216:	Park operations with offices, workshop, garages, storage, and meeting room
Bldg. 225:	Sand/salt
Bldg. 228:	Potable water treatment facility

Concept 3

Concept 3 is an expansion of Concept 2 and, while still intended primarily for the learning center, it would retain most of the existing buildings. This would allow for more educational and research programs in expanded facilities. Buildings not needed by the learning center would be made available for lease for compatible uses.

Learning center programs would be clustered in the center of the current Navy base. Programs would be offered in Building 39 (commissary), where 2 classrooms or laboratories would be located along with an outdoor classroom, and a small office for the learning center. Building 1 (Rockefeller) would provide exhibit space, a small visitor center, and offices for the learning center and its partnership organizations. Building 105 (galley) would provide food service with its full-service kitchen and cafeteria. Other program space would be available in Building 164 (child development center) which would house a small theater and in Building 143 (Schooner Club) which has a kitchen, a classroom and 2 dining or meeting rooms with a capacity of 50 people each. The Navy's history at Schoodic and Mount Desert Island would be interpreted in the original portion of Building 3, which would be restored to its former appearance. Other learning center facilities would be housed in the remaining portions of the building, now the base chapel, including offices and 3 classrooms or laboratories.

The learning center could provide housing for 15-20 researchers and up to 190 students. Students would be housed in Building 84 (dormitory), or in the onsite campground in the summer months. Researchers and park staff would be accommodated in the Schoodic Shores housing complex with 24 two-bedroom apartments and 8 four-bedroom units. Three 2-bedroom cabins would be available for additional overnight lodging and could be leased out by the learning center to gain revenue. The campground and picnic pavilion would remain for learning center use, and a group camping area would be constructed where the ball field is now situated. Building 138 (gymnasium) would be converted into a multi-purpose large assembly space.

Roads, paths, and open space would be reconfigured to create a more efficient and pleasant campus environment.

Park operations would be located in Building 216 (public works), and would include offices, storage, garages, and a meeting room. Archival collections would be stored and maintained in Building 162, now a bowling alley. The number of NPS personnel at Schoodic would depend upon the operational and programmatic needs of the learning center, and would include full-time, permanent maintenance, protection, administrative, and interpretive positions. The current wastewater treatment facility and potable water system, including the water tower, would remain.

Buildings not needed for the learning center and available for lease might include the medical clinic, salt and sand storage, and some housing units.

The system of roads, paths, parking lots, and open space would be reconfigured to create a more efficient and pleasant campus environment. The remaining portions of the disturbed site, once cleared of structures, would be restored to the appropriate native plant community. About 10 acres of disturbed landscape would be restored.

Accommodations would be available for up to 350 people in campsites, cabins, apartments, and dormitories. The learning center might have as many as 600 program users on site on a peak day. Leased office or research space might provide employment for an additional 50 people. The

Schoodic unit of the park would experience a moderate increase in visitor day use, as well as overnight use.

Building Use Summary:

Bldg. 1:   Visitor center, exhibits, book sales, offices
Bldg. 2:   Generator house
Bldg. 3:   Navy interpretive exhibits, offices, and 3 classrooms/laboratories
Bldg. 9:   Gatehouse/visitor contact station
Bldg. 39:   2 classrooms/laboratories, outdoor classroom
Bldg. 45:   Generator house
Bldg. 84:   190 beds for students
Bldg. 105: Food service with full-service kitchen and cafeteria
Bldg. 138: Gymnasium
Bldg. 139: Picnic pavilion to serve 15-site campground and group camping area
Bldg. 141: Water tower
Bldg. 143: 1 classroom, kitchen, 2 meeting rooms
Bldg. 148: Research
Bldg. 162: Curatorial office, research facilities, and archives storage
Bldg. 165: Gas Station
Bldg. 167: Fire Station
Bldg. 183: Wastewater treatment facility
Bldgs. 184-200: Schoodic Shores 32 townhouses for researchers and employees
Bldg. 216: Park operations with offices, workshop, garages, storage, and meeting room
Bldg. 225: Sand/salt storage
Bldg. 228: Potable water treatment facility

APPENDIX B

Ferry Financial Model

Ferry Operator Financial Performance Model

For the purposes of evaluating the relative economic performance of the various ferry route alternatives proposed in this waterborne transportation plan, the financial performance of the different vessel types and operating scenarios is measured by calculating the rate of return on required equity investment over the estimated project life cycle on a discounted cash flow (DCF) basis. The project life cycle refers here to the time period over which a new vessel is introduced and operated, which is based here largely upon reasonable estimates of vessel service life. Even in the case of government subsidized ferry services, minimizing the subsidy amount required to generate a positive return on equity investment is an appropriate measure of the economic performance of the ferry operator, even though the operation might not be considered a strictly commercial enterprise. Therefore, the financial analysis approach outlined below is applicable to a broad spectrum of ferry operations.

The income statement known as a *statement of cash flows* is used here as the basis for determining the return on equity investment on a discounted cash flow basis. A series of annual cash flow statements are estimated for every year of the project life cycle, under the various operating scenarios, using different vessel types and with estimated levels of ridership. The net cash flows before taxes (sometimes referred to as the residual) for each year of the project are then compared to the required equity investment over the project life, all on a discounted basis.

Required equity investment typically includes a portion of the vessel purchase price (i.e., the down payment), start-up expenses and provision of working capital for new routes, and any cash deficits experienced during the project life cycle. Start-up expenses and provision of working capital represent one-time costs associated with the start-up of a completely new service (e.g., marketing and advertising, accounting, legal, permitting, licensing, etc.). This category of required equity investment is discussed in more detail later under the section entitled Indirect Operating Costs.

The stream of annual cash flows is compared to the required equity investment on a discounted basis, resulting in the calculation of the projects internal rate of return (IRR). The internal rate of return is the discount rate or interest rate that equalizes the expected positive cash flows with the negative cash flows (equity investment) of the project. That scenario which yields the greatest internal rate of return provides the greatest return on required equity investment over the project life cycle, and is therefore considered superior in its economic performance to other scenarios that yield lesser internal rates of return.

In keeping with generally accepted principals and methods for the financial analysis of transportation business entities, total expenses (cash outflows) are classified into three mutually exclusive categories of *vessel debt repayment*, *direct operating costs* and *indirect operating costs*. Vessel debt repayment includes principal and interest payments on the portion of the vessel purchase price not funded by the equity investment of the owners. Direct operating costs are defined here as vessel direct operating costs, which are generally considered to include crew costs (in this case deck and engine crew only, excluding passenger service crew), fuel and lubricant costs, hull insurance, and vessel maintenance. Indirect operating costs are defined here as including items that are not included under the direct operating costs category, for example, passenger service crew costs (if applicable), terminal related costs such as passenger facility charges and docking fees, marketing and advertising, and general administration.

In evaluating vessel attributes that affect operator financial performance (e.g., fuel consumption, vessel maintenance, vessel purchase price, etc.), historically observed data were obtained whenever possible from sources such as the current operators of the vessel(s) or operators of similar vessel(s), or vessel designers and shipyards.

In evaluating the economic performance of a particular vessel type and operating scenario, operating and financial data obtained from various ferry operators, as well as data from other ferry service feasibility studies, were used to develop plausible estimates of unit costs that were subsequently utilized in arriving at the estimated annual income statements for each alternatives analysis. Wherever possible, estimates based on actual operating experience were utilized.

Certain cost elements, such as labor expense, and to a lesser extent vessel debt repayment, usually represent a disproportionately large share of total expenses, whereas certain indirect costs elements are quite modest and in some cases relatively insignificant relative to overall expenses. Therefore, when necessary, priority was placed upon obtaining reasonable and accurate estimates for those cost elements that represent the largest share of overall operating costs, since it is here where any variation would result in the greatest relative change in financial performance. Also, for many of the indirect cost categories, it is not clear that there is any basis for assuming that the costs incurred would vary as a function of different vessel types.

Table 0-1 presents the discounted cash flow analysis expense and revenue categories examined for each case study. Unless otherwise noted, all dollar values noted in this report represent year 2000 U.S. dollars.

The definition of each individual element of expense and revenue reviewed, and how each varies as a function of items such as vessel hours, number of passengers, or other factors, is presented in the remainder of this chapter, and follows in the order they are presented in Table 0-1.

Vessel Debt Repayment

Vessel debt repayment represents principal and interest payments on the portion of the vessel purchase price not funded by the equity investment of the owners. Leasing expense, for example under a bareboat charter arrangement, would be an alternative method of accounting for ownership expenses, and in some cases, leasing allows for the indirect realization of certain tax advantages. In many instances, leasing is used primarily as a mechanism for the ferry company to limit its potential liability, in which a

TABLE 0-1: FERRY OPERATOR EXPENSE AND REVENUE CATEGORIES

EXPENSES
Annual Vessel Debt Repayment
Annual Vessel Debt Repayment (combined principal and interest)
Direct Operating Costs
Salaries, Wages and Benefits (Deck and Engine, Officers & Crew)
Vessel Fuel and Lubricants
Vessel Maintenance Costs
Marine Hull Insurance
Indirect Operating Costs
Salaries, Wages and Benefits (Onboard Passenger Service Crew)
Marketing and Advertising
Reservations & Sales
Dockage Fees / Passenger Facility Charges / Shore Operations
Protection and Indemnity (P&I) Insurance
General Administration
Outside Professional Services
Onboard Food & Beverage Sales - Cost of Sales
REVENUES
Passenger Fares
Ancillary Sales - Onboard Food & Beverage Sales
Ancillary Sales - Parking Revenues
Federal, State or Local Operating or Non-Operating Subsidy
NET CASH FLOW BEFORE TAXES
Net Cash Flow Before Taxes

leasing company that is separate from, but related to, the ferry company is set up in order to protect the vessels against any lawsuits that may be brought against the ferry company.

Three possible scenarios are possible with respect to this expense element:

(1) a newly built or existing used vessel may be purchased by the operator in order to provide service on the route being studied

(2) an existing vessel already owned and operated by an operator may be used to provide service on the route

(3) in certain scenarios, it is possible that the proposed vessels will be in excess of 30 years old or older, and therefore perhaps owned outright and fully depreciated, such that ownership cost per se is virtually zero. However, in such cases maintenance and overhaul expenses are often higher than if a newer vessel were to be utilized, and changes to maintenance expense category should be made accordingly.

Regardless of which of these three scenarios is likely to be the case for a given alternatives analysis, unless the vessel in question is used entirely and exclusively only on the ferry route being studied, care must be taken to properly allocate vessel debt repayment expense among the different routes on which the vessel is being operated.[1]

In an attempt to arrive at reasonable purchase price estimates for new vessels, the observed purchase prices for recently acquired vessels of varying types and capacities can be used for guidance. Alternatively, for existing vessels already in operation on other routes by an operator, the amount of existing vessel debt repayment for a given existing vessel could be used as the basis for this expense element.

For the acquisition of a newly built vessel, in industry practice, various vessel financing terms are possible, including various amortization schedules, loan terms, and interest rate amounts and types (fixed, variable, etc.). For vessels receiving a loan guarantee under the Title XI program of the U.S. Maritime Administration (discussed in Appendix D), a minimum ownership equity contribution (down payment) of 12.5% is required, and a level principal, rather than equal payment, amortization schedule is used in almost all cases. This results in larger payment amounts earlier in the loan term, when the interest component is the largest.

Based on a review of available data and discussions with existing ferry operators, purchase prices for *newly built* vessels suitable for serving Acadia National Park are estimated as function of the passenger capacity of the vessel and the vessel hull material, as follows:

Aluminum hull:	$3,950 per passenger seat
Steel hull:	$3,000 per passenger seat
Wood hull:	$2,300 per passenger seat

all of which are expressed in year 2000 dollars. Therefore, for example, for the purposes of this study, a newly built 250 passenger vessel with an aluminum hull would be assumed to have an acquisition price of approximately $987,500.

To estimate the value of a *used vessel*, its value as a new vessel is estimate as above, and is then depreciated by an amount equivalent to 2.3% of the new vessel purchase price annually, for vessels that are 37 years old or younger. For older vessels, 15% of the new vessel price is assumed as the value of the vessel. Therefore, for example, a 15 year old, 250 passenger vessel with a steel hull is estimated to have a current value of $469,000.

To calculate the debt repayment expense in each of the case studies, unless otherwise specified for a particular scenario, an equal payment amortization schedule is assumed, with a required owner equity (down payment) of 20% of the purchase price, a loan term of 15 years, and a fixed interest rate of 10%. Alternatively, for existing vessels already in operation on other routes by an operator, the amount of existing vessel debt repayment for a given existing vessel should be used as the basis for this expense element.

---

[1] For example, if a new vessel is purchased and is to be operated on two separate routes, the total vessel debt repayment expenses should be allocated to each route accordingly, using vessel hours operated on each route as a suitable basis for the allocation.

Direct Operating Costs (DOC)

DOC - Salaries, Wages and Benefits (Deck and Engine, Officers & Crew)

In a typical analysis of direct operating costs for a ferry operation, the total crew complement required for the operation of each vessel is classified into the three functional categories of *deck crew*, *engine crew*, and *passenger service crew*, with the passenger service crew category reviewed later under indirect cost elements. For the purpose of assigning appropriate rates of compensation, both the deck crew and engine crew functional categories are then assigned the further job classifications of either *officer* or *general crew*. Depending upon the vessel type and size, the deck crew labor category typically may include positions such as the captain, deck officers, navigator and other bridge crew, and deckhands. Similarly, the engine crew labor category typically may include a chief engineer, other engineering officers and engineering crew.

For the ferry routes serving this area, vessel sizes, route lengths and the location of the routes in a protected bay result in a relatively simple set of crew labor categories that consist of *captains* and *deck hands*. For vessels that are less than 65 feet in length and have a certificated passenger capacity of 150 passengers or less, one captain and one deck hand are required.

Hourly compensation rates by labor function and job classification represent the cost of salaries, wages and benefits (i.e., fully burdened rates). Total expense for this income statement category is therefore a function of the hourly compensation rate by job function and job classification, vessel operating hours or block hours, plus an additional amount of time equal to 25% of vessel operating hours, added to account for labor time required for vessel preparation and vessel turnaround activities.

For the analysis of ferry routes serving Acadia National Park, fully burdened labor rates of $37.50 per hour are utilized for *captains*, $10.00 per hour for *senior deck hands*, and $6.00 per hour for *deck hands*.

The total crew complement for each labor category and for each vessel type analyzed was determined on the basis of the observed manning requirements of existing vessel types.

DOC - Vessel Fuel and Lubricants

Vessel fuel and lubricant expenses represent the capital, maintenance, and administrative costs associated with the provision of fuel and refueling services, including fuel taxes. For a specific vessel type, total annual fuel and lubricant expense is a function of total vessel hours by operating mode, fuel consumption rate by operating mode, and the unit fuel and lubricant cost. Fuel consumption at idle is accounted for by assuming that vessel hours at idle are equal to 15% of vessel operating hours or block hours.

Route profiles detailing the distance traveled and operating speed over each segment of a route for each vessel type can be used if desired, and are developed using electronic charting software and digital nautical charts. Less detailed route descriptions can also be specified if desired. Fuel consumption rates by vessel and by operating mode (e.g., service speed, intermediate speed, slow speed, idle, etc.) are based on detailed data obtained for existing vessels, with fuel consumption rates for various operating speeds estimated based on vessel powering data and the specific fuel consumption of various marine diesel engine types. The resulting fuel consumption rates by operating mode were then further verified by comparing the resulting estimates to actual data for a sample of ferry vessels that currently serve the area.

There is a wide variety of commercially available diesel fuel oil. Diesel No. 2 (low sulfur) is commonly utilized for ferry vessels, and is assumed here for all analyses. Purchased in bulk at a wholesale price, the price per gallon for Diesel No. 2, including all taxes, was $1.41 in late 2000. Vessel serving cross-bay routes generally require refueling after completing eight round trips, with most vessels having a fuel capacity of between 275 and 600 gallons depending upon the specific vessel.

Based on discussion with shipyards and vessel operators, the quantity of lubricant consumed is assumed to be 0.4% of the quantity of fuel consumption, with the unit cost of lubricant assumed to be $8.00 per gallon.

DOC - Vessel Maintenance Costs

Vessel maintenance expenses represent the cost of vessel hull and engine repairs and preventative maintenance, including periodic replacement of engines and related systems. Maintenance is assumed to be carried out either in-house, or contracted to an outside service provider, with the maintenance expense representing all components of total maintenance cost, including labor, materials and parts, and burden (overhead).

In general, it is thought that maintenance for high speed vessels such as catamarans is more preventative, more proactive, and done more frequently than for conventional vessels. Despite this, maintenance expense for older conventional monohull vessels may not necessarily be less than for a high speed vessel, due in large part to the age of these older vessels and the possibility of more frequent upgrades and overhauls being required.

Whenever possible, observed values for vessel maintenance expense were used, data were obtained on observed maintenance expenditures for similar vessels operating elsewhere, or maintenance cost information provided by shipyards was used.

In order to refine these maintenance costs estimates, and provide estimates for vessels for which limited data was available, the existing data were reconciled and combined into the following maintenance cost estimation methodology, based in part upon maintenance cost methodologies used in other ferry service feasibility studies.

Total annual maintenance expense per vessel is hypothesized to be partially dependent upon total vessel hours per year, especially for engine maintenance. Based on the observed data, total annual vessel maintenance expense for a new vessel is estimated to be equal to 3.5% of the purchase price of the purchase price of the vessel, for a vessel operating a nominal 1,000 hours annually. To account for variation in total annual maintenance expense resulting from different levels of annual vessel operating hours and different vessel ages, the following formula is then used to estimate total annual maintenance expenses for a vessel:

$$[M * F * P] + [(M * V * P) * (H_a / H_n)]$$

M = estimated total annual maintenance cost for new vessel, expressed as a percentage of the
new vessel purchase price
F = percent of maintenance cost that is fixed (does not vary with vessel hours)
P = new vessel purchase price
V = percent of maintenance cost that varies with vessel hours
H_a = actual annual vessel hours operated
H_n = nominal annual vessel hours (1,000 hours)

In this formula, 60% of total maintenance expenses is essentially fixed, with the remainder varying as a function of total vessel hours, with nominal annual vessel hours assumed to be 1,000. For a vessel operated less than 1,000 hours annually, total maintenance expense is reduced somewhat, and above 1,000 hours, it is increased. Note that the resulting value for vessel maintenance, expressed as a per hour rate, may actually be less for higher operating hours, since although total maintenance expense increases, it increases at a slower rate than do total annual operating hours, resulting in somewhat lower hourly figures for maintenance.

Finally, to account for variations in maintenance expense resulting from the age of a vessel, the result of the above formula is then increased for each year of vessel age by a value equal to 2% of the new vessel annual maintenance expense, for each year of vessel age. Therefore, a ten year old vessel would have an annual maintenance expense that is 20% more than that for a similar new vessel.

DOC - Marine Hull Insurance

Hull insurance primarily represents property insurance coverage for the vessel and equipment, although it often includes collision liability coverage for damage to other vessels and their cargo as well. In determining insurance premiums, a variety of factors are usually taken into consideration. These include: (1) size of vessel, (2) age of vessel, (3) hull value, (4) area of navigation, (5) years of operating experience, (6) completion of USCG safety courses, and (7) extent of fire protection equipment on the vessel. Although high speed craft do not currently seem to have a substantially greater insurance risk than conventional vessels, some industry observers agree that the risk issues with high speed craft are different than with conventional vessels, and that the insurance underwriting market has yet to fully assess high speed craft for the potential risks that may be associated with them.[2]

Based on discussion with ferry operators, policies are treated here as "actual cash value" policies, which pay the depreciated value of the vessel, rather than the full replacement value of a new vessel, in the event of a loss. The hull insurance expense element is calculated here as a function of the current estimated value of the vessel. The current value of the vessel is estimated as described earlier in Section 0, "Vessel Debt Repayment," and assumes that vessels are depreciated by an amount equivalent to 2.3% of the new vessel purchase price annually. Estimates obtained from shipyards, existing ferry operators, and other ferry service feasibility studies suggest that annual marine hull

---

[2] *Fast Ferry International.* July-August 1997. Page 21.

insurance expense typically equals between 1% to 3% of the value of the vessel being insured. A value of 2% of the vessel value is used here as a reasonable estimate of annual hull insurance expense.

Indirect Operating Costs (IOC)

As noted earlier in the discussion of required equity investment, although not applicable to many of the alternative scenarios evaluated as part of the National Park Service studies currently being conducted by the Volpe Center, start-up expenses and provision of working capital represent one-time costs associated with the start-up of a completely new service (e.g., marketing and advertising, accounting, legal, permitting, licensing, etc.). Where applicable, start-up expense and provision of working capital for completely new ferry operators and services are assumed to equal 11% of total year 3 (equilibrium patronage) passenger revenues, including any ancillary revenues, and is assumed to be provided from owner equity in year zero (before project start-up).

IOC - Salaries, Waves and Benefits (Onboard Passenger Service Crew)

As noted earlier, the total crew complement required for the operation of each vessel is classified into the three functional categories of *deck crew*, *engine crew*, and *passenger service crew*, with the deck crew and engine crew categories reviewed earlier under direct cost elements. Depending upon the vessel type, size, and typical voyage length, the passenger service crew category may include positions such as cabin attendants, pursers, and stewards, although for the scenarios evaluated as part of the National Park Service studies currently being conducted by the Volpe Center, would be limited to staff engaged primarily in the onboard sales of food and beverage, if applicable. In most if not all scenarios, such duties may be carried out deck crew members in addition to their other tasks, and therefore there would be no dedicated onboard passenger service crew.

As with deck and engine crew, hourly compensation rates for passenger service crew represent the cost of salaries, wages and benefits (i.e., fully burdened rates). Total expense for this income statement category is therefore a function of the hourly compensation rate, vessel operating hours or block hours, plus an additional amount of time equal to 25% of vessel operating hours, added to account for labor time required for vessel preparation and vessel turnaround activities.

IOC - Marketing and Advertising

This indirect cost category represents the production and distribution of marketing materials and costs associated with the purchase of print, radio, television or other media advertising. This category is of particular importance to new startup services in creating awareness and building ridership. Based on previous ferry feasibility studies, this expense category is assumed to vary as a function of total passenger revenues, including ancillary revenues (and thus indirectly as a function of total ridership), and to be equal to 2% of these revenues. For a completely new operator and route, a higher value of 4% of these revenues is more appropriate.

IOC - Reservations & Sales

This cost category includes labor costs of reservations and sales personal, and commissions costs, or direct charges arising from sales of passenger tickets. Based on previous ferry feasibility studies, this expense category is assumed to vary as a function of passenger revenues (and thus indirectly as a function of total ridership), and to be equal to 1.5% of passenger revenues.

IOC - Dockage Fees / Passenger Facility Charges / Shore Operations

For ferry terminal facilities owned by the ferry operator, shore operations costs represent the direct and indirect costs to the ferry operator (terminal operator) of operating, manning (e.g., ticket sales, etc.), maintaining, insuring, and providing security for the terminal facilities. For ferry terminal facilities owned by another party (a port authority, municipality, private entity, etc.), shore operations costs are typically reflected as a terminal usage fee, often assessed as a flat annual fee or a per passenger charge, and in some cases a vessel docking fee that is often assessed per foot of vessel length. For each case study, the specific method of calculating total expenses for this cost category may vary based on whether the shore facilities are owned by the ferry operator or not, and the manner in which terminal usage fees are assessed (e.g., as an annual fixed fee, or as a per passenger boarding charge). For the Acadia National Park analyses, dockage fee are assessed at a zero to minimal rate because the operator is assumed to own the docks or pay very small charges.

IOC - Protection and Indemnity (P&I) Insurance

This expense category includes insurance against passenger liability, crew liability, and other liabilities (which often include liquor liability, pollution liability, premises liability and medical payments). P&I covers a wide range of liability exposures and miscellaneous expenses that a vessel owner might incur. Injuries to crew members and other persons on board the insured vessel are generally the most common claims. Coverage is typically provided for injury to persons aboard other vessels struck by the insured vessel, and for damage to property (other than vessels) struck by the insured vessel. Accidental pollution from the discharge of fuel oil or other similar substances is also often covered, unless due to negligence by the operator.

Based on previous ferry feasibility studies, this expense category is assumed to vary as a function of the number of passengers carried, and to be equal to $0.35 per passenger boarding.

IOC - General Administration

This expense category represents costs of a general corporate nature that are incurred in performing activities which contribute to more than a single operating function. Specific examples include leasing of office space, telephone & communications costs, office supplies, travel, and management and administrative personnel compensation and benefits.

Based on previous ferry feasibility studies and information from ferry operators including those currently serving the Mount Desert Island area, this expense category is assumed to be equal to a fixed annual amount of $5,000, plus an additional amount equal to $0.50 per passenger boarding

IOC - Outside Professional Services

This cost may vary as a function of the total number of passengers depending on the service, no cost is allocated here.

IOC - Onboard Food & Beverage Sales - Cost of Sales

Although not applicable to most of the alternative scenarios evaluated as part of the National Park Service studies currently being conducted by the Volpe Center, the financial performance model can accommodate scenarios in which ancillary revenues are earned from onboard food and beverage sales. This cost category represents the costs associated with the purchase of supplies and onboard food and beverage sales operations. Based on previous ferry feasibility studies and standard food service industry practice, it is assumed here that the cost of sales for onboard food and beverage sales is equal to 65% of onboard food and beverage revenues.

Revenues

Revenues - Passenger Fares

Passenger fares are the primary source of revenue for all routes, and revenues from the sale of advertising space either onboard the vessel or at the ferry terminals is not considered here, since even in transportation operations where this practice tends to be widespread (e.g., bus and rail public transit), revenues received from advertising are only a small fraction of overall revenues. The model can accommodate a full adult fare, as well as a discount fare level (e.g., adult, child). If one-way fares of an amount reater than half of the round trip fare are charged and make up a significant portion of passenger fare revenues, then the model can be modified to accommodate this scenario if necessary. Similarly, if more complex multi-trip discount ticket scenarios are necessary, the model can be modified to accommodate this as well.

Revenues - Ancillary Sales - Onboard Food & Beverage Sales

Although not applicable to most of the alternative scenarios evaluated as part of the National Park Service studies currently being conducted by the Volpe Center, the financial performance model can accommodate scenarios in which ancillary revenues are earned from onboard food and beverage sales. This revenue category represents revenues from food and beverage sales, including bar sales of liquor and vending machine revenues, if applicable. This revenue category is assumed to vary as a function of total passenger boardings, and can be specified at various amounts depending upon experience in similar or related routes or markets.

Revenues - Parking Revenues

For ferry operators who maintain ownership and control of parking facilities at or near their ferry terminals and at which ferry passengers will park their vehicles for a fee, parking revenues may contribute significantly to the financial viability of a proposed ferry route or service. In order to properly calculate the magnitude of these revenues, an estimate must be made both of the mode of ground access to the ferry terminal for patrons of the new ferry service, and of the length of stay of these passengers. Consideration must also be given, however, to the fact that necessary capacity must be available at the parking facilities in order to accommodate the number of vehicles that would result during the seasons, days of week, or times of day being studied.

Revenues - Federal, State or Local Operating or Non-Operating Subsidy

If applicable, the financial performance model can accommodate scenarios in which federal, state or local operating or non-operating subsidies are provided for the service. As noted earlier, for government subsidized ferry services such as these, minimizing the total net cost (the difference between total revenues and total expenses), and thus the required subsidy, is an appropriate measure of the economic performance of the ferry operator even though the operation might not be considered a strictly commercial enterprise.

Net Cash Flow Before Taxes

The net cash flow before taxes is the total revenues earned by the ferry operator, net of expenses and before taxes, and represents a summary measure of the financial performance of the operator under a given operating scenario for a particular year of the project period. Negative values for annual net cash flow before taxes are, by implication, considered here to be additional funds provided by the equity investors to cover these cash deficits. Net cash flow is considered here before taxes largely as a matter of convenience, since the explicit incorporation of the many federal, state and local taxes which a ferry operator would be subject to extends beyond the scope of this study. Also, for the comparative operational analyses for which this financial performance model is meant to be applied, it is assumed that the exclusion of taxes, though perhaps affecting the absolute financial performance of various alternative analyses, will not significantly affect the relative financial performance of these alternative analyses to any significant extent.

APPENDIX C

Population and Employment Data and Forecasts

County	Town	Population Forecasts			
		1990	2000	2005	2015
Hancock	Amhurst	227	238	244	255
Hancock	Aurora	82	86	88	93
Hancock	Blue Hill	1,948	2,044	2,092	2,190
Hancock	Brooklin	788	827	846	886
Hancock	Brooksville	763	800	819	858
Hancock	Bucksport	4,841	5,081	5,201	5,445
Hancock	Castine	1,165	1,223	1,251	1,310
Hancock	Cranberry Isles	190	199	204	213
Hancock	Dedham	1,233	1,294	1,325	1,387
Hancock	Deer Isle	1,835	1,926	1,972	2,064
Hancock	Eastbrook	290	304	312	326
Hancock	Ellsworth	5,995	6,292	6,441	6,742
Hancock	Franklin	1,145	1,202	1,230	1,288
Hancock	Frenchboro	44	46	47	50
Hancock	Great Pond	59	62	64	67
Hancock	Hancock	1,942	2,038	2,086	2,183
Hancock	Lamoine	1,315	1,381	1,413	1,479
Hancock	Mariaville	271	284	291	305
Hancock	Orland	1,811	1,901	1,946	2,037
Hancock	Osborn	72	76	78	81
Hancock	Otis	356	374	383	401
Hancock	Penobscot	1,135	1,191	1,219	1,276
Hancock	Sedgwick	908	953	976	1,021
Hancock	Sorrento	296	311	318	333
Hancock	Southwest Harbor	1,959	2,056	2,104	2,203
Hancock	Stonington	1,256	1,318	1,350	1,413
Hancock	Surry	1,007	1,057	1,082	1,133
Hancock	Swans Island	349	366	375	393
Hancock	Tremont	1,328	1,394	1,427	1,494
Hancock	Trenton	1,064	1,116	1,143	1,196
Hancock	Verona	517	542	555	581
Hancock	Waltham	277	291	298	311
Hancock	Gouldsboro	1,993	2,091	2,141	2,241
Hancock	Sullivan	1,122	1,177	1,205	1,262
Hancock	Winter Harbor	1,161	1,218	1,247	1,306
Hancock	Bar Harbor	4,458	4,679	4,789	5,014
Hancock	Mount Desert	1,905	2,000	2,047	2,143
Hancock County Total		47,107	49,441	50,607	52,977

County	Town	Population Forecasts			
		1990	2000	2005	2015
Washington	Addison	1,118	1,173	1,201	1,257
Washington	Beals	669	702	719	753
Washington	Cherryfield	1,187	1,246	1,275	1,335
Washington	Columbia	438	460	471	493
Washington	Columbia Falls	554	581	595	623
Washington	Harrington	896	940	963	1,008
Washington	Jonesboro	587	616	631	660
Washington	Jonesport	1,530	1,606	1,644	1,721
Washington	Machias	2,578	2,705	2,769	2,899
Washington	Machiasport	1,170	1,228	1,257	1,316
Washington	Milbridge	1,309	1,374	1,407	1,473
Washington	Steuben	1,088	1,142	1,168	1,223
Washington	Alexander	480	503	515	539
Washington	Baileyville	2,038	2,139	2,189	2,292
Washington	Baring	276	290	296	310
Washington	Beddington	43	45	46	49
Washington	Calias	3,976	4,173	4,272	4,472
Washington	Centerville	30	32	32	34
Washington	Charlotte	272	285	292	306
Washington	Codyville	35	37	38	39
Washington	Cooper	124	131	134	140
Washington	Crawford	89	94	96	100
Washington	Cutler	782	820	840	879
Washington	Danforth	712	748	765	801
Washington	Deblois	73	77	79	82
Washington	Dennysville	356	374	383	401
Washington	E. Machias	1,222	1,283	1,313	1,374
Washington	Eastport	1,972	2,069	2,118	2,217
Washington	Grand Lake Stream plant.	175	183	188	196
Washington	Lubec	1,859	1,951	1,997	2,091
Washington	Marshfield	463	485	497	520
Washington	Meddybemps	133	140	143	150
Washington	Northfield	99	104	107	112
Washington	Passamaquoddy Indian Township	619	650	665	696
Washington	Passamaquoddy Pleasant Point	574	602	617	645
Washington	Pembroke	855	897	918	961
Washington	Perry	761	798	817	855
Washington	Princeton	976	1,025	1,049	1,098
Washington	Robbinson	497	521	534	559
Washington	Roque Bluffs	235	246	252	264
Washington	Talmadge	62	65	67	70
Washington	Topsfield	236	247	253	265
Washington	Unorganized	1,161	1,218	1,247	1,306
Washington	Vanceboro	202	212	217	227
Washington	Waite	119	125	128	134
Washington	Wesley	146	154	157	165
Washington	Whiting	408	429	439	459
Washington	Whitneyville	242	254	260	272
County Total		35,428	37,183	38,060	39,842

County	Town	Employment Forecasts			
		1990	2000	2005	2015
Hancock	Amhurst	15	18	19	20
Hancock	Aurora	55	65	68	72
Hancock	Blue Hill	1,591	1,884	1,985	2,102
Hancock	Brooklin	306	362	382	404
Hancock	Brooksville	174	206	217	230
Hancock	Bucksport	3,460	4,099	4,318	4,573
Hancock	Castine	603	714	752	797
Hancock	Cranberry Isles	61	72	76	80
Hancock	Dedham	114	135	142	150
Hancock	Deer Isle	492	583	614	651
Hancock	Eastbrook	79	93	98	104
Hancock	Ellsworth	8,248	9,771	10,295	10,901
Hancock	Franklin	179	212	223	236
Hancock	Frenchboro	15	18	19	20
Hancock	Great Pond	15	18	19	20
Hancock	Hancock	501	594	626	663
Hancock	Lamoine	164	194	204	216
Hancock	Mariaville	38	45	47	50
Hancock	Orland	529	626	660	699
Hancock	Osborn	58	68	72	76
Hancock	Otis	36	43	45	48
Hancock	Penobscot	338	400	422	446
Hancock	Sedgwick	164	194	204	216
Hancock	Sorrento	35	41	43	46
Hancock	Southwest Harbor	1,351	1,601	1,686	1,786
Hancock	Stonington	659	781	822	871
Hancock	Surry	206	244	257	272
Hancock	Swans Island	103	122	129	136
Hancock	Tremont	354	420	442	468
Hancock	Trenton	248	294	310	328
Hancock	Verona	62	74	78	82
Hancock	Waltham	6	7	8	8
Hancock	Gouldsboro	766	908	957	1,013
Hancock	Sullivan	359	425	448	474
Hancock	Winter Harbor	217	257	270	286
Hancock	Bar Harbor	4,684	5,549	5,846	6,190
Hancock	Mount Desert	1,141	1,351	1,424	1,508
Hancock County Total		**27,424**	**32,488**	**34,229**	**36,246**

County	Towns	Employment Forecasts			
		1990	2000	2005	2015
Washington	Addison	176	208	219	232
Washington	Beals	148	176	185	196
Washington	Cherryfield	442	524	552	585
Washington	Columbia	153	181	191	202
Washington	Columbia falls	201	239	251	266
Washington	Harrington	258	305	321	340
Washington	Jonesboro	214	253	267	282
Washington	Jonesport	464	549	579	613
Washington	Machias	3260	3862	4069	4308
Washington	Machiasport	189	224	236	250
Washington	Milbridge	723	856	902	955
Washington	Steuben	83	99	104	110
Washington	Alexander	36	43	45	48
Washington	Baileyville	2413	2859	3012	3189
Washington	Baring	108	127	134	142
Washington	Beddington	29	34	36	38
Washington	Calias	3386	4011	4226	4475
Washington	Centerville	0	0	0	0
Washington	Charlotte	50	59	62	66
Washington	Codyville	0	0	0	0
Washington	Cooper	15	18	19	20
Washington	Crawford	2	2	2	2
Washington	Cutler	48	57	61	64
Washington	Danforth	432	511	539	571
Washington	Deblois	118	140	147	156
Washington	Dennysville	26	31	32	34
Washington	E. Machias	461	546	575	609
Washington	Eastport	1198	1419	1496	1584
Washington	Grand Lake Stream plant.	12	14	15	16
Washington	Lubec	894	1059	1115	1181
Washington	Marshfield	5	5	6	6
Washington	Meddybemps	24	29	30	32
Washington	Northfield	2	2	2	2
Washington	Passamaquoddy Indian Township	303	359	378	400
Washington	Passamaquoddy Pleasant Point	258	305	321	340
Washington	Pembroke	118	140	147	156
Washington	Perry	308	364	384	406
Washington	Princeton	357	424	446	472
Washington	Robbinson	24	29	30	32
Washington	Roque Bluffs	12	14	15	16
Washington	Talmadge	0	0	0	0
Washington	Topsfield	33	39	42	44
Washington	Unorganized	454	538	567	601
Washington	Vanceboro	52	61	64	68
Washington	Waite	91	108	113	120
Washington	Wesley	47	56	59	62
Washington	Whiting	44	52	55	58
Washington	Whitneyville	21	25	26	28
County Total		**17,690**	**20,956**	**22,079**	**23,380**

County	Towns	1990	2000	2005 (Low)	2005 (High)	2015 (Low)	2015 (High)
JTW - Destination Bar Harbor, Mount Desert Island							
Hancock	Amhurst		-		-	-	
Hancock	Aurora		-			-	
Hancock	Blue Hill	2	2	2	3	-	
Hancock	Brooklin		-			-	
Hancock	Brooksville		-			-	
Hancock	Bucksport	12	14	14	15	-	
Hancock	Castine	2	2	2	3	-	
Hancock	Cranberry Isles	3	5	5	6	3	5
Hancock	Dedham	4	5	5	5	-	
Hancock	Deer Isle	5	7	7	8	2	3
Hancock	Eastbrook	10	12	12	13	1	6
Hancock	Ellsworth	216	262	276	291	32	55
Hancock	Franklin	57	66	69	73	3	9
Hancock	Frenchboro		-			-	
Hancock	Great Pond		-			-	
Hancock	Hancock	73	91	96	101	15	34
Hancock	Lamoine	68	82	87	92	10	21
Hancock	Mariaville	8	11	11	12	3	5
Hancock	Orland	8	9	9	10	-	
Hancock	Osborn	3	3	4	4	-	
Hancock	Otis	9	10	11	11	-	
Hancock	Penobscot	2	2	2	3	-	
Hancock	Sedgwick	8	9	9	10	-	
Hancock	Sorrento	5	6	6	6	-	
Hancock	Southwest Harbo	190	240	253	267	45	77
Hancock	Stonington		-			-	
Hancock	Surry	33	44	46	48	11	19
Hancock	Swans Island		-			-	
Hancock	Tremont	177	224	236	249	43	81
Hancock	Trenton	134	163	171	181	20	34
Hancock	Verona		-			-	
Hancock	Waltham		-			-	
Hancock	Gouldsboro	19	24	25	26	4	377
Hancock	Sullivan	23	27	29	30	2	33
Hancock	Winter Harbor	8	9	9	10	-	108
Hancock	Bar Harbor	1,877	2,172	2,288	2,411	98	169
Hancock	Mount Desert	700	1,045	1,101	1,160	441	753
Hancock Total		3,656	4,545	4,789	5,046	733	1,790

County	Towns	1990	2000	2005 (Low)	2005 (High)	2015 (Low)	2015 (High)
	JTW - Destination Bar Harbor, Mount Desert Island						
Washington	Addison	2	2	2	3	-	6
Washington	Beals		-			-	5
Washington	Cherryfield	2	2	2	3	-	8
Washington	Columbia		-			-	3
Washington	Columbia Falls		-			-	4
Washington	Harrington	8	11	11	12	3	14
Washington	Jonesboro	4	5	5	5		-
Washington	Jonesport		-			-	9
Washington	Machias	2	3	4	4	2	3
Washington	Machiasport		-			-	
Washington	Milbridge	9	10	11	11	-	27
Washington	Steuben	9	11	12	13	2	39
Washington	Alexander		-			-	
Washington	Baileyville		-			-	
Washington	Baring		-			-	
Washington	Beddington		-			-	
Washington	Calias		-			-	
Washington	Centerville		-			-	
Washington	Charlotte		-			-	
Washington	Codyville		-			-	
Washington	Cooper		-			-	
Washington	Crawford		-			-	
Washington	Cutler		-			-	
Washington	Danforth		-			-	
Washington	Deblois		-			-	
Washington	Dennysville		-			-	
Washington	E. Machias		-			-	
Washington	Eastport		-			-	
Washington	Grand Lake Strea		-			-	
Washington	Lubec		-			-	
Washington	Marshfield		-			-	
Washington	Meddybemps		-			-	
Washington	Northfield		-			-	
Washington	Passamaquoddy		-			-	
Washington	Passamaquoddy		-			-	
Washington	Pembroke		-			-	
Washington	Perry		-			-	
Washington	Princeton		-			-	
Washington	Robbinson		-			-	
Washington	Roque Bluffs		-			-	
Washington	Talmadge		-			-	
Washington	Topsfield		-			-	
Washington	Unorganized		-			-	
Washington	Vanceboro		-			-	
Washington	Waite		-			-	
Washington	Wesley		-			-	
Washington	Whiting		-			-	
Washington	Whitneyville		-			-	
Washington Total		36	45	47	50	7	119

	Journey to Work -- Destination: Winter Harbor/Gouldsboro						
County	Towns	1990	2000	2005 (Low)	2005 (High)	2015 (Low)	2015 (High)
Hancock	Amhurst				-		
Hancock	Aurora				-		
Hancock	Blue Hill				-		
Hancock	Brooklin				-		
Hancock	Brooksville				-		
Hancock	Bucksport				-		
Hancock	Castine				-		
Hancock	Cranberry Isles				-		
Hancock	Dedham				-		
Hancock	Deer Isle				-		
Hancock	Eastbrook	4	5	5	5		
Hancock	Ellsworth	20	22	23	29	51	59
Hancock	Franklin	6	7	7	8	5	6
Hancock	Frenchboro				-		
Hancock	Great Pond				-		
Hancock	Hancock	13	15	16	18	13	15
Hancock	Lamoine	4	5	5	5		
Hancock	Mariaville		-				
Hancock	Orland				-		
Hancock	Osborn				-		
Hancock	Otis				-		
Hancock	Penobscot				-		
Hancock	Sedgwick				-		
Hancock	Sorrento	9	10	11	13	23	27
Hancock	Southwest Harbor				-		
Hancock	Stonington				-		
Hancock	Surry	1	1	1	1	3	3
Hancock	Swans Island				-		
Hancock	Tremont	8	9	10	10		
Hancock	Trenton				-		
Hancock	Verona				-		
Hancock	Waltham				-		
Hancock	Gouldsboro	665	652	687	771	611	604
Hancock	Sullivan	60	68	71	82	76	88
Hancock	Winter Harbor	470	375	396	470	712	668
Hancock	Bar Harbor	10	11	12	14	20	24
Hancock	Mount Desert				-		
Hancock Total		1,270	1,179	1,243	1,427	1,514	1,493

APPENDIX D

Park Visitation Data and Forecasts

Acadia National Park Recreational Visits (Source: NPS Website)

	Jan.	Feb.	Mar.	Apr.	May	Jun.	Jul.	Aug.	Sep.	Oct.	Nov.	Dec.	Yearly
1990	16,084	13,383	30,060	71,898	148,090	290,533	554,953	645,522	355,864	207,770	47,633	11,801	2,393,591
1991	24,588	14,667	31,291	75,738	157,252	295,348	574,529	640,990	377,904	224,497	45,518	13,535	2,475,857
1992	17,510	21,110	30,312	63,276	164,400	262,173	539,109	615,843	391,798	211,573	46,316	18,693	2,382,113
1993	19,402	15,556	29,040	57,707	192,823	300,647	586,449	719,671	417,317	254,615	43,755	19,052	2,656,034
1994	13,364	18,112	29,086	58,788	182,781	311,803	617,622	720,079	421,106	268,779	48,907	20,322	2,710,749
1995	14,894	20,510	32,120	86,198	175,550	355,270	626,947	753,799	439,553	271,606	54,121	14,810	2,845,378
1996	17,655	15,576	32,452	76,597	166,290	327,723	571,017	714,090	426,562	280,577	56,828	19,464	2,704,831
1997	16,292	17,230	27,035	77,005	132,194	340,064	622,847	758,140	404,808	287,171	57,810	19,710	2,760,306
1998	16,726	17,028	27,500	81,896	148,052	307,208	565,477	701,097	391,378	266,138	55,225	16,772	2,594,497
1999	16,430	17,162	33,688	82,993	174,610	315,980	562,996	639,073	426,024	277,644	39,416	16,211	2,602,227
2000	22,500	23,848	35,423	78,555	166,456	319,208	547,929	594,904	378,135	253,626	33,693	14,961	2,469,238
11 Year Total	195,445	194,182	338,007	810,651	1,808,498	3,425,957	6,369,875	7,503,208	4,430,449	2,803,996	529,222	185,331	28,594,821
Yearly Average	17,768	17,653	30,728	73,696	164,409	311,451	579,080	682,110	402,768	254,909	48,111	16,848	2,599,529
2005	18,003	17,887	31,135	69,698	166,587	315,578	586,753	691,148	408,105	258,286	48,749	17,072	2,629,000
2015	20,407	20,275	35,292	79,003	188,829	357,711	665,090	783,424	462,591	292,770	55,257	19,351	2,980,000

1

Acadia Park Recreational Visits: Distribution by Month (Source: NPS website)

	Jan.	Feb.	Mar.	Apr.	May	Jun.	Jul.	Aug.	Sep.	Oct.	Nov.	Dec.	Yearly
1990	0.67%	0.56%	1.26%	3.00%	6.19%	12.14%	23.18%	26.97%	14.87%	8.68%	1.99%	0.49%	100%
1991	0.99%	0.59%	1.26%	3.06%	6.35%	11.93%	23.21%	25.89%	15.26%	9.07%	1.84%	0.55%	100%
1992	0.74%	0.89%	1.27%	2.66%	6.90%	11.01%	22.63%	25.85%	16.45%	8.88%	1.94%	0.78%	100%
1993	0.73%	0.59%	1.09%	2.17%	7.26%	11.32%	22.08%	27.10%	15.71%	9.59%	1.65%	0.72%	100%
1994	0.49%	0.67%	1.07%	2.17%	6.74%	11.50%	22.78%	26.56%	15.53%	9.92%	1.80%	0.75%	100%
1995	0.52%	0.72%	1.13%	3.03%	6.17%	12.49%	22.03%	26.49%	15.45%	9.55%	1.90%	0.52%	100%
1996	0.65%	0.58%	1.20%	2.83%	6.15%	12.12%	21.11%	26.40%	15.77%	10.37%	2.10%	0.72%	100%
1997	0.59%	0.62%	0.98%	2.79%	4.79%	12.32%	22.56%	27.47%	14.67%	10.40%	2.09%	0.71%	100%
1998	0.64%	0.66%	1.06%	3.16%	5.71%	11.84%	21.80%	27.02%	15.08%	10.26%	2.13%	0.65%	100%
1999	0.63%	0.66%	1.29%	3.19%	6.71%	12.14%	21.64%	24.56%	16.37%	10.67%	1.51%	0.62%	100%
2000	0.91%	0.97%	1.43%	3.18%	6.74%	12.93%	22.19%	24.09%	15.31%	10.27%	1.36%	0.61%	100%
11 Year Ave.	0.68%	0.68%	1.18%	2.83%	6.32%	11.98%	22.28%	26.24%	15.49%	9.81%	1.85%	0.65%	100%
2005	0.68%	0.68%	1.18%	2.65%	6.34%	12.00%	22.32%	26.29%	15.52%	9.82%	1.85%	0.65%	100%
2015	0.68%	0.68%	1.18%	2.65%	6.34%	12.00%	22.32%	26.29%	15.52%	9.82%	1.85%	0.65%	100%

APPENDIX D

2

Schoodic Parkland Recreational Visits by Month (Source: NPS website) (Growth Matches Acadia)

	Jan.	Feb.	Mar.	Apr.	May	Jun.	Jul.	Aug.	Sep.	Oct.	Nov.	Dec.	Yearly
1990	3,096	4,056	6,036	10,802	18,414	25,704	41,814	51,264	31,824	18,594	8,786	3,336	223,726
1991	4,733	4,445	6,283	11,379	19,553	26,130	43,289	50,904	33,795	20,091	8,396	3,826	232,824
1992	3,370	6,398	6,087	9,507	20,442	23,195	40,620	48,907	35,037	18,934	8,543	5,284	226,325
1993	3,735	4,715	5,831	8,670	23,976	26,599	44,187	57,153	37,320	22,786	8,071	5,386	248,427
1994	2,572	5,489	5,840	8,832	22,728	27,586	46,536	57,185	37,658	24,054	9,021	5,745	253,247
1995	2,867	6,216	6,450	12,950	21,828	31,431	47,239	59,863	39,308	24,307	9,983	4,187	266,629
1996	3,398	4,721	6,516	11,508	20,677	28,994	43,024	56,709	38,146	25,110	10,482	5,502	254,789
1997	3,136	5,222	5,429	11,569	16,437	30,086	46,930	60,208	36,201	25,700	10,663	5,572	257,152
1998	3,220	5,161	5,522	12,304	18,409	27,179	42,607	55,677	35,000	23,818	10,186	4,741	243,824
1999	3,163	5,201	6,764	12,469	21,712	27,955	42,420	50,752	38,098	24,847	7,270	4,583	245,235
2000	4,331	7,228	7,113	11,802	20,698	28,241	41,285	47,244	33,816	22,698	6,215	4,229	234,899
11 Year Total	37,621	58,851	67,871	121,793	224,875	303,101	479,950	595,866	396,204	250,939	97,616	52,391	2,687,077
11 Year Ave.	3,420	5,350	6,170	11,072	20,443	27,555	43,632	54,170	36,019	22,813	8,874	4,763	244,280
2005	3,465	5,421	6,252	10,471	20,714	27,920	44,210	54,887	36,496	23,115	8,992	4,826	246,769
2015	3,928	6,145	7,087	11,870	23,480	31,647	50,113	62,215	41,368	26,201	10,192	5,470	279,716

APPENDIX D

APPENDIX E

Base Reuse Data and Forecasts

Schoodic Navy Base Reuse Plan: 2005 Employment & Visitation

Average Daily Trip Making Activity by Reuse Scenario		Concept 1				Concept 3			
		Summer		Winter		Summer		Winter	
		Employees	Visitors	Employees	Visitors	Employees	Visitors	Employees	Visitors
Bldg 1									
	Admin	20	10	15	3	20	10	15	3
	Research	20	7	10	3	20	7	10	3
	Library	5	5	2	1	5	5	2	1
	Vistor Ctr	5	90	0	0	5	180	1	0
Bldg 3									
	Navy Museum	0	0	0	0	2	30	0	0
	Classrooms	0	0	0	0	2	30	0	0
Bldg 39									
	Classroom	0	0	0	0	2	40	2	10
Bldg 84									
	Dormitory	1	20	1	20	2	20	1	20
	Classroom	4	60	1	0	7	90	2	0
Bldg 105									
	Cafeteria	5	1	2	1	6	2	3	1
Bldg 138									
	Assembly Hall	0	0	0	0	2	50	1	10
Bldg 143									
	Meeting Space	0	0	0	0	2	50	1	10
Bldg 162									
	Archives	0	0	0	0	1	4	1	0
Bldg 164									
	Theater	0	0	0	0	2	20	0	0
Bldg 216									
	Park HQ	10	7	4	2	30	10	10	7
Campsites		0	0	0	0	2	45	1	0
Leased Office Space		0	0	0		50	7	50	5
Totals		70	200	35	30	160	600	100	70

Schoodic Navy Base Reuse Plan: 2015 Employment & Visitation at the Base									
Average Daily		Concept 1				Concept 3			
Trip Making Activity		Summer		Winter		Summer		Winter	
by Reuse Scenario		Employees	Visitors	Employees	Visitors	Employees	Visitors	Employees	Visitors
Bldg 1									
	Admin	20	10	15	3	20	10	15	3
	Research	20	7	10	3	20	7	10	3
	Library	5	5	2	1	5	5	2	1
	Vistor Ctr	5	130	0	0	5	220	1	0
Bldg 3									
	Navy Museum	0	0	0	0	2	30	0	0
	Classrooms	0	0	0	0	2	30	0	0
Bldg 39									
	Classroom	0	0	0	0	2	40	2	10
Bldg 84									
	Dormitory	1	20	1	20	2	20	1	20
	Classroom	4	60	1	0	7	90	2	0
Bldg 105									
	Cafeteria	5	1	2	1	6	2	3	1
Bldg 138									
	Assembly Hall	0	0	0	0	2	50	1	10
Bldg 143									
	Meeting Space	0	0	0	0	2	50	1	10
Bldg 162									
	Archives	0	0	0	0	1	4	1	0
Bldg 164									
	Theater	0	0	0	0	2	20	0	0
Bldg 216									
	Park HQ	10	7	4	2	30	10	10	7
Campsites		0	0	0	0	2	60	1	0
Leased Office Space		0	0	0		50	7	50	5
Totals		70	240	35	30	160	655	100	70

APPENDIX F

Ferry Service Schedules, Demand and Patronage Data,
Service Costs, and Revenues

78' Catamaran schedules

Schedule I - **summer - weekdays**

Winter Harbor Leave	Bar Harbor Arrive	Bar Harbor Leave	Winter Harbor Arrive
Morning			
5:15 AM	5:36 AM	5:51 AM	6:12 AM
6:27 AM	6:48 AM	7:03 AM	7:25 AM
7:40 AM	8:01 AM	9:00 AM	9:21 AM
9:45 AM	10:06 AM	10:30 AM	10:51 AM
11:15 AM	11:36 AM		
Afternoon		12:00 PM	12:21 PM
1:45 PM	2:06 PM	2:30 PM	2:51 PM
3:06 PM	3:27 PM	3:42 PM	4:03 PM
4:18 PM	4:40 PM	4:55 PM	5:16 PM
5:31 PM	5:52 PM	6:07 PM	6:29 PM
6:44 PM	7:05 PM	7:20 PM	7:41 PM

comm. one ways	10	rec. one ways	10
total one ways	20		

Schedule II - **summer - weekends**

Winter Harbor Leave	Bar Harbor Arrive	Bar Harbor Leave	Winter Harbor Arrive
Morning			
8:00 AM	8:21 AM	8:36 AM	8:57 AM
9:12 AM	9:33 AM	9:48 AM	10:10 AM
10:25 AM	10:46 AM	11 01 AM	11:22 AM
11:37 AM	11:59 AM	12:14 PM	12:35 PM
Afternoon			
12:50 PM	1:11 PM	1:26 PM	1:48 PM
2:03 PM	2:24 PM	2:39 PM	3:00 PM
3:15 PM	3:37 PM	3:52 PM	4:13 PM
4:28 PM	4:49 PM	5:04 PM	5:26 PM
5:41 PM	6:02 PM	6:17 PM	6:38 PM
6:53 PM	7:14 PM	7:29 PM	7:51 PM

comm. one ways	7	rec. one ways	13
total one ways	20		

Schedule III - **winter - weekdays**

Winter Harbor Leave	Bar Harbor Arrive	Bar Harbor Leave	Winter Harbor Arrive
Morning			
5:15 AM	5:36 AM	5:51 AM	6:12 AM
6:27 AM	6:48 AM	7:03 AM	7:25 AM
7:40 AM	8:01 AM	9:30 AM	9:51 AM
11:00 AM	11:21 AM		
Afternoon		12:30 PM	12:51 PM
2:00 PM	2:21 PM	3:30 PM	3:51 PM
4:06 PM	4:27 PM	4:42 PM	5:03 PM
5:18 PM	5:40 PM	5:55 PM	6:16 PM
6:31 PM	6:52 PM	7:07 PM	7:29 PM

comm. one ways	10	rec. one ways	6
total one ways	16		

Schedule IV - **winter - weekends**

Winter Harbor Leave	Bar Harbor Arrive	Bar Harbor Leave	Winter Harbor Arrive
Morning			
8:00 AM	8:21 AM	8:36 AM	8:57 AM
10:00 AM	10:21 AM	10:36 AM	10:57 AM
11:12 AM	11:33 AM	11:48 AM	12:10 PM
Afternoon			
1:00 PM	1:21 PM	1:36 PM	1:57 PM
3:00 PM	3:21 PM	3:36 PM	3:57 PM

comm. one ways	4	rec. one ways	6
total one ways	10		

2 x 50' Monohull schedules

Schedule I - **summer - weekdays**

Winter Harbor Leave	Bar Harbor Arrive	Bar Harbor Leave	Winter Harbor Arrive
Morning			
5:15 AM	5:40 AM	5:15 AM	5:40 AM
5:55 AM	6:20 AM	5:55 AM	6:20 AM
6:35 AM	7:00 AM	6:35 AM	7:00 AM
7:15 AM	7:40 AM	7:15 AM	7:40 AM
7:55 AM	8:20 AM	7:55 AM	8:20 AM
8:35 AM	9:00 AM	8:35 AM	9:00 AM
10 00 AM	10:25 AM	10:00 AM	10:25 AM
10:40 AM	11:05 AM	10:40 AM	11:05 AM
Afternoon			
12 00 PM	12:25 PM	12:00 PM	12:25 PM
12:40 PM	1:05 PM	12:40 PM	1:05 PM
2:00 PM	2:25 PM	2:00 PM	2:25 PM
2:40 PM	3:05 PM	2:40 PM	3:05 PM
3:20 PM	3:45 PM	3:20 PM	3:45 PM
4:00 PM	4:25 PM	4:00 PM	4:25 PM
4:40 PM	5:05 PM	4:40 PM	5:05 PM
5:20 PM	5:45 PM	5:20 PM	5:45 PM
6:00 PM	6:25 PM	6:00 PM	6:25 PM
6:40 PM	7:06 PM	6:40 PM	7:06 PM
7:21 PM	7:46 PM	7:21 PM	7:46 PM

comm. one ways	20	rec. one ways	18
total one ways	38		

Schedule II - **summer - weekends**

Winter Harbor Leave	Bar Harbor Arrive	Bar Harbor Leave	Winter Harbor Arrive
Morning			
8:00 AM	8:25 AM	8:00 AM	8:25 AM
8:40 AM	9:05 AM	8:40 AM	9:05 AM
10:00 AM	10:25 AM	10 00 AM	10:25 AM
10:40 AM	11:05 AM	10:40 AM	11:05 AM
Afternoon			
12:00 PM	12:25 PM	12 00 PM	12:25 PM
12:40 PM	1:05 PM	12:40 PM	1:05 PM
2:00 PM	2:25 PM	2:00 PM	2:25 PM
2:40 PM	3:05 PM	2:40 PM	3:05 PM
5:00 PM	5:25 PM	5:00 PM	5:25 PM
5:40 PM	6:05 PM	5:40 PM	6:05 PM
6:20 PM	6:45 PM	6:20 PM	6:45 PM
7:00 PM	7:25 PM	7:00 PM	7:25 PM

comm. one ways	8	rec. one ways	16
total one ways	24		

Schedule III - **winter - weekdays**

Winter Harbor Leave	Bar Harbor Arrive	Bar Harbor Leave	Winter Harbor Arrive
Morning			
5:15 AM	5:40 AM	5:15 AM	5:40 AM
5:55 AM	6:20 AM	5:55 AM	6:20 AM
6:35 AM	7:00 AM	6:35 AM	7:00 AM
7:15 AM	7:40 AM	7:15 AM	7:40 AM
7:55 AM	8:20 AM	7:55 AM	8:20 AM
8:35 AM	9:00 AM	8:35 AM	9:00 AM
Afternoon			
11 00 AM	11:25 AM	11:00 AM	11:25 AM
11:40 AM	12:05 PM	11:40 AM	12:05 PM
2:00 PM	2:25 PM	2:00 PM	2:25 PM
2:40 PM	3:05 PM	2:40 PM	3:05 PM
3:30 PM	3:55 PM	3:30 PM	3:55 PM
4:10 PM	4:35 PM	4:10 PM	4:35 PM
4:50 PM	5:15 PM	4:50 PM	5:15 PM
5:30 PM	5:55 PM	5:30 PM	5:55 PM

Schedule IV - **winter - weekends**

Winter Harbor Leave	Bar Harbor Arrive	Bar Harbor Leave	Winter Harbor Arrive
Morning			
8:00 AM	8:25 AM	8:00 AM	8:25 AM
11:00 AM	11:25 AM	11 00 AM	11:25 AM
11:40 AM	12:05 PM	11:40 AM	12:05 PM
Afternoon			
1:00 PM	1:25 PM	1:00 PM	1:25 PM
3:00 PM	3:25 PM	3:00 PM	3:25 PM
4:00 PM	4:25 PM	4:00 PM	4:25 PM

PRIMARY MODEL INPUTS, 50' MONOHULL

Vessel Related Inputs	
Vessel Name	Expeditions II
Number of vessels required	1
Total number of vessel one-way trips annually	3,536
Passenger capacity	64
Vessel length in feet	50.2
Vessel Hull Material Type	Aluminum
Vessel age in years	8

Vessel Ownership Cost Inputs	
New ALUMINUM HULL Vessel Purchase Price PER PASSENGER SEAT (Year 2000 US$)	$3,950
New STEEL HULL Vessel Purchase Price PER PASSENGER SEAT (Year 2000 US$)	$3,000
New WOOD HULL Vessel Purchase Price PER PASSENGER SEAT (Year 2000 US$)	$2,300
Annual Straight-Line Depreciation (% of New Vessel Price) to Estimate Used Vessel Price (	2.3%
Value of Used Vessel that is 38 years old or older (as a % of New Vessel Price)	15.0%
Estimated NEW VESSEL PURCHASE PRICE, per vessel (Year 2000 US$)	$610,000
Estimated Current DEPRECIATED Value of the Vessel (Year 2000 US$)	$497,760
Percent Vessel Debt Repayment Allocated to this route	60.0%
Vessel owner equity / down payment as a percent of purchase price	20.0%
Interest rate	10.00%
Loan period / anticipated useful vessel life (years)	15
Amortization schedule (equal payment or equal principal)	equal payment

Vessel Maintenance Costs	
Annual Maintenance Cost per vessel (at a nominal 3,000 operating hours annually) as a %	2.50%
Portion of Annual Maintenance Cost that is "fixed"	60.00%
Portion of Annual Maintenance Cost that varies with respect to total annual operating hours	40.00%
Nominal Annual Vessel Operating Hours	1,000
Additional maintenance expense for used vessels for each year of age (as a % of new vess	2.00%
Annual NEW Vessel Maintenance Expense (for the observed number of operating hours pe	$18,137
Annual ACTUAL Vessel Maintenance Expense	$21,039

Fuel Consumption Rates by Operating Mode (gallons per hour at indicated speed)	
GPH at service speed	49
GPH at Low Speed #4	23
GPH at Low Speed #3	16
GPH at Low Speed #2	14
GPH at Low Speed #1	12
GPH at idle	11
Lubricant Consumption in gallons as a percent of fuel consumption in gallons	0.4%

Vessel Operating Hours (Total and by Mode of Operation)	
Vessel Service Speed (knots)	22
Annual Vessel Operating Hours at Idle, as a percent of total operating hours	15.0%
Total Annual Vessel Operating Hours	1,473
Annual Vessel Operating Hours at Service Speed	1,120
Annual Vessel Operating Hours at Low Speed #4	0
Annual Vessel Operating Hours at Low Speed #3	354
Annual Vessel Operating Hours at Low Speed #2	0
Annual Vessel Operating Hours at Low Speed #1	0
Annual Vessel Operating Hours at Idle	221

PRIMARY MODEL INPUTS, 50' MONOHULL (CONT'D.)

Patronage Related Inputs	
Total number of annual one-way passenger seats available	226,304
Total number of annual passenger boardings (equilibrium years 3 through 25)	47,320
Percent total passenger boardings at full adult fare	86.8%
Percent total passener boardings at discount fare (child, senior)	13.2%
Year 1 ridership as a percent of equilibrium year 3 ridership	100.0%
Year 2 ridership as a percent of equilibrium year 3 ridership	100.0%
Passenger capacity utilization rate	20.91%
Percent of passengers participating in onboard gaming	0.0%
Passenger Facilities Charges per passenger boarding at Terminal #1	$0.10
Passenger Facilities Charges per passenger boarding at Terminal #2	$0.10
Docking Fee per Foot of vessel length at Terminal #1	$0.00
Docking Fee per Foot of vessel length at Terminal #2	$0.00
Unit Economic Values	
Diesel fuel price per gallon	$1.41
Lubricant price per gallon	$8.00
Adult ONE-WAY passenger fare (including pfc's, but not departure taxes)	$0.00
Discount (child, senior) ONE-WAY fare as a percent of full adult one-way fare	60.0%
Discount (child, senior) one-way passenger fare (including pfc's, but not departure taxes)	$0.00
Total Crew Complement by Function and Job Classification	
Captains	1
Senior Deck Hands	0
Deck Hands	1
Engine Crew	0
Onboard Passenger Service Crew	0
Total Crew Complement	2
Crew Hourly Compensation by Function and Job Classification (fully burdened rates)	
Non-block time crew hours, as a percent of total vessel operating hours (e.g., vessel turnarc	25.0%
Captain hourly pay rate	$37.50
Senior Deck Hand hourly pay rate	$10.00
Deck Hand hourly pay rate	$6.00
Engine Crew hourly pay rate	$31.73
Passenger Service Crew hourly pay rate	$14.44
Cost Model Coefficients	
"Marine Hull Insurance" annual cost as a percent of vessel current vessel value	2.0%
"Marketing & Advertising" expense as a percent of total revenues	2.0%
"Reservations & Sales" as a percent of passenger & vehicle fare revenues	1.5%
"P&I Insurance" cost per passenger	$0.35
Onboard food and beverage revenue per passenger	$0.00
Onboard food and beverage cost of sales, as a percent of food & beverage revenues	65.0%
Gift shop revenue per passenger	$0.00
Gift shop cost of sales, as a percent of gift shop revenues	45.0%
Onboard Gaming revenue per participating passenger	$0.00
Percent of total passengers participating in onboard gaming	0.0%
Onboard Gaming cost of sales, as a percent of Onboard Gaming revenues	50.0%
Onetime Start-Up Costs for new operations, as a percent of Year 3 total fare and ancillary s	0.0%
Interest rate at which onetime start-up expenses are amortized at	10.0%
Loan period (years) over which the onetime start-up expenses are amortized	5
Fixed annual amount for "General Administration" expense	$5,000
"General Administration" cost per passenger boarding	$0.50
Intercept term for the linear model estimating the per passenger "Outside Profession Servic	0
"Outside Professional Services" expense per passenger boarding	$0.00

PRIMARY MODEL INPUTS, 78' CATAMARAN

Vessel Related Inputs	
Vessel Name	Evercrest
Number of vessels required	1
Total number of vessel one-way trips annually	3,640
Passenger capacity	100
Vessel length in feet	78.7
Vessel Hull Material Type	Aluminum
Vessel age in years	2

Vessel Ownership Cost Inputs	
New ALUMINUM HULL Vessel Purchase Price PER PASSENGER SEAT (Year 2000 US$)	$3,950
New STEEL HULL Vessel Purchase Price PER PASSENGER SEAT (Year 2000 US$)	$3,000
New WOOD HULL Vessel Purchase Price PER PASSENGER SEAT (Year 2000 US$)	$2,300
Annual Straight-Line Depreciation (% of New Vessel Price) to Estimate Used Vessel Price (	2.3%
Value of Used Vessel that is 38 years old or older (as a % of New Vessel Price)	15.0%
Estimated NEW VESSEL PURCHASE PRICE, per vessel (Year 2000 US$)	$1,200,000
Estimated Current DEPRECIATED Value of the Vessel (Year 2000 US$)	$1,144,800
Percent Vessel Debt Repayment Allocated to this route	60.0%
Vessel owner equity / down payment as a percent of purchase price	20.0%
Interest rate	10.00%
Loan period / anticipated useful vessel life (years)	15
Amortization schedule (equal payment or equal principal)	equal payment

Vessel Maintenance Costs	
Annual Maintenance Cost per vessel (at a nominal 3,000 operating hours annually) as a %	3.50%
Portion of Annual Maintenance Cost that is "fixed"	60.00%
Portion of Annual Maintenance Cost that varies with respect to total annual operating hours	40.00%
Nominal Annual Vessel Operating Hours	1,000
Additional maintenance expense for used vessels for each year of age (as a % of new vess	2.00%
Annual NEW Vessel Maintenance Expense (for the observed number of operating hours pe	$50,680
Annual ACTUAL Vessel Maintenance Expense	$52,707

Fuel Consumption Rates by Operating Mode (gallons per hour at indicated speed)	
GPH at service speed	80
GPH at Low Speed #4	22
GPH at Low Speed #3	22
GPH at Low Speed #2	20
GPH at Low Speed #1	18
GPH at idle	18
Lubricant Consumption in gallons as a percent of fuel consumption in gallons	0.4%

Vessel Operating Hours (Total and by Mode of Operation)	
Vessel Service Speed (knots)	27
Annual Vessel Operating Hours at Idle, as a percent of total operating hours	15.0%
Total Annual Vessel Operating Hours	1,517
Annual Vessel Operating Hours at Service Speed	1,153
Annual Vessel Operating Hours at Low Speed #4	0
Annual Vessel Operating Hours at Low Speed #3	364
Annual Vessel Operating Hours at Low Speed #2	0
Annual Vessel Operating Hours at Low Speed #1	0
Annual Vessel Operating Hours at Idle	228

PRIMARY MODEL INPUTS, 78' CATAMARAN (CONT'D.)

Patronage Related Inputs	
Total number of annual one-way passenger seats available	364,000
Total number of annual passenger boardings (equilibrium years 3 through 25)	51,324
Percent total passenger boardings at full adult fare	86.8%
Percent total passener boardings at discount fare (child, senior)	13.2%
Year 1 ridership as a percent of equilibrium year 3 ridership	100.0%
Year 2 ridership as a percent of equilibrium year 3 ridership	100.0%
Passenger capacity utilization rate	14.10%
Percent of passengers participating in onboard gaming	0.0%
Passenger Facilities Charges per passenger boarding at Terminal #1	$0.10
Passenger Facilities Charges per passenger boarding at Terminal #2	$0.10
Docking Fee per Foot of vessel length at Terminal #1	$0.00
Docking Fee per Foot of vessel length at Terminal #2	$0.00
Unit Economic Values	
Diesel fuel price per gallon	$1.41
Lubricant price per gallon	$8.00
Adult ONE-WAY passenger fare (including pfc's, but not departure taxes)	$10.00
Discount (child, senior) ONE-WAY fare as a percent of full adult one-way fare	60.0%
Discount (child, senior) one-way passenger fare (including pfc's, but not departure taxes)	$6.00
Total Crew Complement by Function and Job Classification	
Captains	1
Senior Deck Hands	0
Deck Hands	1
Engine Crew	0
Onboard Passenger Service Crew	0
Total Crew Complement	2
Crew Hourly Compensation by Function and Job Classification (fully burdened rates)	
Non-block time crew hours, as a percent of total vessel operating hours (e.g., vessel turnarc	25.0%
Captain hourly pay rate	$37.50
Senior Deck Hand hourly pay rate	$10.00
Deck Hand hourly pay rate	$6.00
Engine Crew hourly pay rate	$31.73
Passenger Service Crew hourly pay rate	$14.44
Cost Model Coefficients	
"Marine Hull Insurance" annual cost as a percent of vessel current vessel value	2.0%
"Marketing & Advertising" expense as a percent of total revenues	2.0%
"Reservations & Sales" as a percent of passenger & vehicle fare revenues	1.5%
"P&I Insurance" cost per passenger	$0.35
Onboard food and beverage revenue per passenger	$0.00
Onboard food and beverage cost of sales, as a percent of food & beverage revenues	65.0%
Gift shop revenue per passenger	$0.00
Gift shop cost of sales, as a percent of gift shop revenues	45.0%
Onboard Gaming revenue per participating passenger	$0.00
Percent of total passengers participating in onboard gaming	0.0%
Onboard Gaming cost of sales, as a percent of Onboard Gaming revenues	50.0%
Onetime Start-Up Costs for new operations, as a percent of Year 3 total fare and ancillary s	0.0%
Interest rate at which onetime start-up expenses are amortized at	10.0%
Loan period (years) over which the onetime start-up expenses are amortized	5
Fixed annual amount for "General Administration" expense	$5,000
"General Administration" cost per passenger boarding	$0.50
Intercept term for the linear model estimating the per passenger "Outside Profession Servic	0
"Outside Professional Services" expense per passenger boarding	$0.00

50' Monohull, Seasonal Operation	2005 High	2005 Low	2015 High	2015 Low
Vessel Debt Service	$ 37,757	$ 37,757	$ 37,757	$ 37,757
Direct Operating Costs				
Salaries, Wages and Benefits	$ 80,113	$ 80,113	$ 80,113	$ 80,113
Vessel Fuel and Lubricants	$ 89,885	$ 89,885	$ 89,885	$ 89,885
Vessel Maintenance Costs	$ 21,039	$ 21,039	$ 24,667	$ 24,667
Marine Hull Insurance	$ 5,973	$ 5,973	$ 4,758	$ 4,758
Direct Operating Costs Subtotal	$ 197,010	$ 197,010	$ 199,422	$ 199,422
Indirect Operating Costs				
Marketing and Advertising	$ 15,491	$ 9,424	$ 18,539	$ 11,550
Reservations & Sales	$ 11,618	$ 7,068	$ 13,904	$ 8,663
Docking Fees / Passenger Facility Charges / Shore Operations	$ 8,757	$ 5,486	$ 10,590	$ 6,750
Protection and Indemnity (P&I) Insurance	$ 30,649	$ 19,201	$ 37,066	$ 23,624
General Administration	$ 48,784	$ 32,430	$ 57,952	$ 38,748
Indirect Operating Costs Subtotal	$ 115,299	$ 73,609	$ 138,052	$ 89,335
Revenue- passenger fares	$774,548	$471,212	$926,944	$577,524
Net Annual Cash Flow Before Taxes	$424,482	$162,836	$551,713	$251,010

50' Monohull, Year Round Operation	2005 High	2005 Low	2015 High	2015 Low
Vessel Debt Service	$ 62,929	$ 62,929	$ 62,929	$ 62,929
Direct Operating Costs				
Salaries, Wages and Benefits	$ 139,019	$ 139,019	$ 139,019	$ 139,019
Vessel Fuel and Lubricants	$ 155,977	$ 155,977	$ 155,977	$ 155,977
Vessel Maintenance Costs	$ 28,705	$ 28,705	$ 33,654	$ 33,654
Marine Hull Insurance	$ 9,955	$ 9,955	$ 7,930	$ 7,930
Direct Operating Costs Subtotal	$ 333,656	$ 333,656	$ 336,580	$ 336,580
Indirect Operating Costs				
Marketing and Advertising	$ 16,564	$ 10,178	$ 19,626	$ 12,477
Reservations & Sales	$ 12,423	$ 7,633	$ 14,720	$ 9,358
Docking Fees / Passenger Facility Charges / Shore Operations	$ 9,692	$ 6,231	$ 11,577	$ 7,669
Protection and Indemnity (P&I) Insurance	$ 33,923	$ 21,809	$ 40,518	$ 26,842
General Administration	$ 53,462	$ 36,156	$ 62,884	$ 43,345
Indirect Operating Costs Subtotal	$ 126,064	$ 82,007	$ 149,325	$ 99,691
Revenue- passenger fares	$828,207	$508,895	$981,315	$623,860
Net Annual Cash Flow Before Taxes	$305,559	$30,304	$432,482	$124,661

(2) X 50' Monohull, Seasonal Operation	2005 High	2005 Low	2015 High	2015 Low
Vessel Debt Service	$ 75,515	$ 75,515	$ 75,515	$ 75,515
Direct Operating Costs				
Salaries, Wages and Benefits	$ 134,306	$ 134,306	$ 134,306	$ 134,306
Vessel Fuel and Lubricants	$ 150,689	$ 150,689	$ 150,689	$ 150,689
Vessel Maintenance Costs	$ 38,706	$ 38,706	$ 45,379	$ 45,379
Marine Hull Insurance	$ 11,946	$ 11,946	$ 9,516	$ 9,516
Direct Operating Costs Subtotal	$ 335,647	$ 335,647	$ 339,891	$ 339,891
Indirect Operating Costs				
Marketing and Advertising	$ 18,468	$ 11,288	$ 21,952	$ 13,768
Reservations & Sales	$ 13,851	$ 8,466	$ 16,464	$ 10,326
Docking Fees / Passenger Facility Charges / Shore Operations	$ 10,416	$ 6,540	$ 12,449	$ 8,008
Protection and Indemnity (P&I) Insurance	$ 36,455	$ 22,890	$ 43,571	$ 28,028
General Administration	$ 57,078	$ 37,700	$ 67,244	$ 45,040
Indirect Operating Costs Subtotal	$ 136,266	$ 86,884	$ 161,679	$ 105,170
Revenue- passenger fares	$923,376	$564,396	$1,097,588	$688,400
Net Annual Cash Flow Before Taxes	**$375,948**	**$66,350**	**$520,503**	**$167,824**

(2) 50' Monohulls, Year Round Operation	2005 High	2005 Low	2015 High	2015 Low
Vessel Debt Service	$ 125,858	$ 125,858	$ 125,858	$ 125,858
Direct Operating Costs				
Salaries, Wages and Benefits	$ 230,913	$ 230,913	$ 230,913	$ 230,913
Vessel Fuel and Lubricants	$ 259,080	$ 259,080	$ 259,080	$ 259,080
Vessel Maintenance Costs	$ 51,277	$ 51,277	$ 60,118	$ 60,118
Marine Hull Insurance	$ 19,910	$ 19,910	$ 15,861	$ 15,861
Direct Operating Costs Subtotal	$ 561,180	$ 561,180	$ 565,971	$ 565,971
Indirect Operating Costs				
Marketing and Advertising	$ 19,738	$ 12,178	$ 23,509	$ 14,853
Reservations & Sales	$ 14,803	$ 9,133	$ 17,632	$ 11,140
Docking Fees / Passenger Facility Charges / Shore Operations	$ 11,514	$ 7,410	$ 13,837	$ 9,070
Protection and Indemnity (P&I) Insurance	$ 40,299	$ 25,936	$ 48,430	$ 31,744
General Administration	$ 62,570	$ 42,052	$ 74,186	$ 50,349
Indirect Operating Costs Subtotal	$ 148,924	$ 96,709	$ 177,593	$ 117,156
Revenue- passenger fares	$986,878	$608,891	$1,175,449	$742,660
Net Annual Cash Flow Before Taxes	**$150,916**	**-$174,856**	**$306,027**	**-$66,325**

78' Catamaran, Seasonal Operation	2005 High	2005 Low	2015 High	2015 Low
Vessel Debt Service	$ 74,277	$ 74,277	$ 74,277	$ 74,277
Direct Operating Costs				
Salaries, Wages and Benefits	$ 82,469	$ 82,469	$ 82,469	$ 82,469
Vessel Fuel and Lubricants	$ 150,489	$ 150,489	$ 150,489	$ 150,489
Vessel Maintenance Costs	$ 52,707	$ 52,707	$ 62,843	$ 62,843
Marine Hull Insurance	$ 13,738	$ 13,738	$ 10,943	$ 10,943
Direct Operating Costs Subtotal	$ 299,402	$ 299,402	$ 306,744	$ 306,744
Indirect Operating Costs				
Marketing and Advertising	$ 17,878	$ 10,798	$ 21,124	$ 13,269
Reservations & Sales	$ 13,408	$ 8,099	$ 15,843	$ 9,952
Docking Fees / Passenger Facility Charges / Shore Operations	$ 10,140	$ 6,282	$ 12,012	$ 7,727
Protection and Indemnity (P&I) Insurance	$ 35,490	$ 21,986	$ 42,042	$ 27,045
General Administration	$ 55,700	$ 36,408	$ 65,060	$ 43,636
Indirect Operating Costs Subtotal	$ 132,616	$ 83,572	$ 156,080	$ 101,630
Revenue- passenger fares	$893,880	$539,900	$1,056,180	$663,460
Net Annual Cash Flow Before Taxes	**$387,585**	**$82,649**	**$519,079**	**$180,810**

78' Catamaran, Year Round Operation	2005 High	2005 Low	2015 High	2015 Low
Vessel Debt Service	$ 123,795	$ 123,795	$ 123,795	$ 123,795
Direct Operating Costs				
Salaries, Wages and Benefits	$ 141,375	$ 141,375	$ 141,375	$ 141,375
Vessel Fuel and Lubricants	$ 257,981	$ 257,981	$ 257,981	$ 257,981
Vessel Maintenance Costs	$ 71,635	$ 71,635	$ 85,411	$ 85,411
Marine Hull Insurance	$ 22,896	$ 22,896	$ 18,239	$ 18,239
Direct Operating Costs Subtotal	$ 493,887	$ 493,887	$ 503,006	$ 503,006
Indirect Operating Costs				
Marketing and Advertising	$ 19,126	$ 11,664	$ 22,632	$ 14,319
Reservations & Sales	$ 14,345	$ 8,748	$ 16,974	$ 10,739
Docking Fees / Passenger Facility Charges / Shore Operations	$ 11,238	$ 7,139	$ 13,367	$ 8,757
Protection and Indemnity (P&I) Insurance	$ 39,333	$ 24,988	$ 46,786	$ 30,648
General Administration	$ 61,190	$ 40,697	$ 71,837	$ 48,784
Indirect Operating Costs Subtotal	$ 145,232	$ 93,235	$ 171,596	$ 113,246
Revenue- passenger fares	$956,302	$583,199	$1,131,623	$715,927
Net Annual Cash Flow Before Taxes	**$193,389**	**-$127,718**	**$333,226**	**-$24,119**

COMMUTERS: Mode Split Demand Calculations by Ferry Service Automobile

Commuter	Off-Season	Daily	Seasonal	Daily				-0.30	-0.40	0.04		Seasonal	
Sources of Trips	Ridership	Ridership	Ridership	Ridership	IVTT	Freq	Elast-Rid	Elast-IVTT	Elast-Freq	Elast-Rid	Induced	Demand	MS=8%
Bar Harbor Bound Trips													
2005-Low-m1	2,340	18	3,120	24	25	40	26	0.99	0.91	23.59	0		
2005-Low-c1	2,730	21	3,640	28	21	32	26	1.05	1.00	27.17	0		
2005-Low-m2	2,730	21	3,640	28	27	24	26	0.97	1.12	28.27	0		
2005-Low-Avg		20		26	24	32						325	26
2005-High-m1	2,340	18	3,120	24	25	40	26	0.99	0.91	23.59	0		
2005-High-c1	2,730	21	3,640	28	21	32	26	1.05	1.00	27.17	0		
2005-High-m2	2,730	21	3,640	28	27	24	26	0.97	1.12	28.27	0		
2005-High-Avg		20		26	24	32						325	26
2015-Low-m1	2,828	22	3,770	29	25	40	30	0.99	0.91	27.22	0		
2015-Low-c1	3,120	24	4,160	32	21	32	30	1.05	1.00	31.35	0		
2015-Low-m2	3,218	25	4,290	33	27	24	30	0.97	1.12	32.62	0		
2015-Low-Avg		23		30	24	32						375	30
2015-High-m1	3,120	24	4,160	32	25	40	34	0.99	0.91	30.84	32		
2015-High-c1	3,608	28	4,810	37	21	32	34	1.05	1.00	35.53	37		
2015-High-m2	3,705	29	4,940	38	27	24	34	0.97	1.12	36.97	38		
2015-High-Avg		26		34	24	32						425	34
Schoodic Bound Trips													
2005-Low-m1	202	2	650	5	25	40	5	0.99	0.91	4.54	0		
2005-Low-c1	202	2	650	5	21	32	5	1.05	1.00	5.23	0		
2005-Low-m2	202	2	650	5	27	24	5	0.97	1.00	4.87	0		
2005-Low-Avg		2		5	24	32						63	5
2005-High-m1	363	3	1,170	9	25	40	10	0.99	0.91	9.07	0		
2005-High-c1	484	4	1,560	12	21	32	10	1.05	1.00	10.45	0		
2005-High-m2	403	3	1,300	10	27	24	10	0.97	1.00	9.73	0		
2005-High-Avg		3		10	24	32						125	10
2015-Low-m1	322	2	1,040	8	25	40	9	0.99	0.91	8.16	0		
2015-Low-c1	363	3	1,170	9	21	32	9	1.05	1.00	9.41	0		
2015-Low-m2	363	3	1,170	9	27	24	9	0.97	1.00	8.76	0		
2015-Low-Avg		3		9	24	32						113	9
2015-High-m1	403	3	1,300	10	25	40	11	0.99	0.91	9.98	10		
2015-High-c1	484	4	1,560	12	21	32	11	1.05	1.00	11.50	12		
2015-High-m2	443	3	1,430	11	27	24	11	0.97	1.00	10.71	11		
2015-High-Avg		3		11	24	32						138	11

m1 = one mono hull   m2 = two mono hulls   Low = Concept 1 of the Base Reuse

c1 = one catamaran   High = Concept 3 of the Base Reuse

APPENDIX F

RECREATIONAL: Mode Split Demand Calculations by Ferry Service & Automobile

Recreational Sources of Trips	Off-Season Ridership	Daily Ridership	Seasonal Ridership	Daily Ridership	IVTT	Freq	Elast-Rid	-0.30 Elast-IVTT	-0.40 Elast-Freq	Elast-Rid	0.04 Induced	Seasonal Demand	MS=8%
Schoodic Bound Trips													
2005-Low-m1	1,001	8	20,020	110	25	40	121	0.99	0.91	109.77	0.00		
2005-Low-c1	1,147	9	22,932	126	21	32	121	1.05	1.00	126.46	0.00		
2005-Low-m2	1,201	9	24,024	132	27	24	121	0.97	1.12	131.58	0.00		
2005-Low-Avg		8		121	24	32						1,513	121
2005-High-m1	1,556	12	31,122	171	25	40	188	0.99	0.91	170.55	0.00		
2005-High-c1	1,793	14	35,854	197	21	32	188	1.05	1.00	196.49	0.00		
2005-High-m2	1,856	14	37,128	204	27	24	188	0.97	1.12	204.44	0.00		
2005-High-Avg		13		188	24	32						2,350	188
2015-Low-m1	1,192	9	23,842	131	25	40	144	0.99	0.91	130.63	0.00		
2015-Low-c1	1,374	11	27,482	151	21	32	144	1.05	1.00	150.50	0.00		
2015-Low-m2	1,429	11	28,574	157	27	24	144	0.97	1.12	156.59	0.00		
2015-Low-Avg		10		144	24	32						1,800	144
2015-High-m1	1,756	14	35,126	193	25	40	213	0.99	0.91	193.23	201		
2015-High-c1	2,020	16	40,404	222	21	32	213	1.05	1.00	222.62	232		
2015-High-m2	2,102	16	42,042	231	27	24	213	0.97	1.12	231.63	241		
2015-High-Avg		15		213	24	32						2,663	213
Bar Harbor Bound Trips													
2005-Low-m1	182	1	3,640	20	25	40	22	0.99	0.91	19.96	0.00		
2005-Low-c1	209	2	4,186	23	21	32	22	1.05	1.00	22.99	0.00		
2005-Low-m2	218	2	4,368	24	27	24	22	0.97	1.12	23.92	0.00		
2005-Low-Avg		2		22	24	32						275	22
2005-High-m1	419	3	8,372	46	25	40	51	0.99	0.91	46.27	0.00		
2005-High-c1	482	4	9,646	53	21	32	51	1.05	1.00	53.30	0.00		
2005-High-m2	501	4	10,010	55	27	24	51	0.97	1.12	55.46	0.00		
2005-High-Avg		4		51	24	32						638	51
2015-Low-m1	255	2	5,096	28	25	40	31	0.99	0.91	28.12	0.00		
2015-Low-c1	291	2	5,824	32	21	32	31	1.05	1.00	32.40	0.00		
2015-Low-m2	300	2	6,006	33	27	24	31	0.97	1.12	33.71	0.00		
2015-Low-Avg		2		31	24	32						388	31
2015-High-m1	573	4	11,466	63	25	40	67	0.99	0.91	60.78	63		
2015-High-c1	664	5	13,286	73	21	32	67	1.05	1.00	70.02	73		
2015-High-m2	692	5	13,832	76	27	24	67	0.97	1.12	72.86	76		
2015-High-Avg		5		67	24	32						838	67

m1 = one mono hull   m2 = two mono hulls
c1 = one catamaran

Low = Concept 1 of the Base Reuse
High = Concept 3 of the Base Reuse

APPENDIX F

Acadia National Park Reuse of the Naval Security Group Activity Center on Schoodic Head
Average Yearly Demand for Ferry Service Between Bar Harbor & Winter Harbor

Number of Round Trips by the Round Trip Cost	1 Monohull				1 Catamaran				2 Monohulls			
	$6	$12	$20	Total	$6	$12	$20	Total	$6	$12	$20	Total
Year 2005												
Low-Concept 1	6,312	3,230	21,613	31,155	7,222	3,702	24,772	35,696	7,222	3,878	25,951	37,051
Commuter Trips	6,312	-	-	6,312	7,222	-	-	7,222	7,222	-	-	7,222
Recreational Trips	-	3,230	21,613	24,843	-	3,702	24,772	28,474	-	3,878	25,951	29,829
High-Concept 3	6,993	5,391	36,078	48,462	8,414	6,211	41,564	56,189	8,073	6,434	43,061	57,568
Commuter Trips	6,993	-	-	6,993	8,414	-	-	8,414	8,073	-	-	8,073
Recreational Trips	-	5,391	36,078	41,469	-	6,211	41,564	47,775	-	6,434	43,061	49,495
Year 2015												
Low-Concept 1	7,960	3,950	26,435	38,345	8,813	4,546	30,425	43,784	9,041	4,720	31,589	45,350
Commuter Trips	7,960	-	-	7,960	8,813	-	-	8,813	9,041	-	-	9,041
Recreational Trips	-	3,950	26,435	30,385	-	4,546	30,425	34,971	-	4,720	31,589	36,309
High-Concept 3	8,983	6,360	42,561	57,904	10,462	7,329	49,045	66,836	10,518	7,627	51,041	69,186
Commuter Trips	8,983	-	-	8,983	10,462	-	-	10,462	10,518	-	-	10,518
Recreational Trips	-	6,360	42,561	48,921	-	7,329	49,045	56,374	-	7,627	51,041	58,668

Yearly is based on 52 weeks from January through December

Commuter trips are based on a 5 day work week.

Commuters are charged $6 for a round trip fare based on regular use of service

Recreational users under 10yrs are charged $12 for a roundtrip fare.

Recreational users over 10 yrs are charged $20 for a roundtrip fare.

APPENDIX F

Acadia National Park Reuse of the Naval Security Group Activity Center on Schoodic Head
Average Off-Season Demand for Ferry Service Between Bar Harbor & Winter Harbor

Number of Round Trips by the Round Trip Cost	1 Monohull				1 Catamaran				2 Monohulls			
	$6	$12	$20	Total	$6	$12	$20	Total	$6	$12	$20	Total
Year 2005												
Low-Concept 1	2,542	154	1,029	3,725	2,932	176	1,180	4,288	2,932	184	1,235	4,351
Commuter Trips	2,542	-	-	2,542	2,932	-	-	2,932	2,932	-	-	2,932
Recreational Trips	-	154	1,029	1,183	-	176	1,180	1,356	-	184	1,235	1,419
High-Concept 3	2,703	257	1,718	4,678	3,214	296	1,979	5,489	3,133	306	2,051	5,490
Commuter Trips	2,703	-	-	2,703	3,214	-	-	3,214	3,133	-	-	3,133
Recreational Trips	-	257	1,718	1,975	-	296	1,979	2,275	-	306	2,051	2,357
Year 2015												
Low-Concept 1	3,150	188	1,259	4,597	3,483	216	1,449	5,148	3,581	225	1,504	5,310
Commuter Trips	3,150	-	-	3,150	3,483	-	-	3,483	3,581	-	-	3,581
Recreational Trips	-	188	1,259	1,447	-	216	1,449	1,665	-	225	1,504	1,729
High-Concept 3	3,523	303	2,026	5,852	4,092	349	2,335	6,776	4,148	363	2,431	6,942
Commuter Trips	3,523	-	-	3,523	4,092	-	-	4,092	4,148	-	-	4,148
Recreational Trips	-	303	2,026	2,329	-	349	2,335	2,684	-	363	2,431	2,794

Off-Season is based on 26 weeks from November through April
Commuter trips are based on a 5 day work week.
Commuters are charged $6 for a round trip fare based on regular use of service
Recreational users under 10yrs are charged $12 for a roundtrip fare.
Recreational users over 10 yrs are charged $20 for a roundtrip fare.

Acadia National Park Reuse of the Naval Security Group Activity Center on Schoodic Head
Average Seasonal Demand for Ferry Service Between Bar Harbor & Winter Harbor

Number of Round Trips by the Round Trip Cost	1 Monohull				1 Catamaran				2 Monohulls			
	$6	$12	$20	Total	$6	$12	$20	Total	$6	$12	$20	Total
Year 2005												
Low-Concept 1	**3,770**	**3,076**	**20,584**	**27,430**	**4,290**	**3,525**	**23,593**	**31,408**	**4,290**	**3,693**	**24,717**	**32,700**
Commuter Trips	3,770	-	-	3,770	4,290	-	-	4,290	4,290	-	-	4,290
Recreational Trips	-	3,076	20,584	23,660	-	3,525	23,593	27,118	-	3,693	24,717	28,410
High-Concept 3	**4,290**	**5,134**	**34,360**	**43,784**	**5,200**	**5,915**	**39,585**	**50,700**	**4,940**	**6,128**	**41,010**	**52,078**
Commuter Trips	4,290	-	-	4,290	5,200	-	-	5,200	4,940	-	-	4,940
Recreational Trips	-	5,134	34,360	39,494	-	5,915	39,585	45,500	-	6,128	41,010	47,138
Year 2015												
Low-Concept 1	**4,810**	**3,762**	**25,176**	**33,748**	**5,330**	**4,330**	**28,976**	**38,636**	**5,460**	**4,495**	**30,085**	**40,040**
Commuter Trips	4,810	-	-	4,810	5,330	-	-	5,330	5,460	-	-	5,460
Recreational Trips	-	3,762	25,176	28,938	-	4,330	28,976	33,306	-	4,495	30,085	34,580
High-Concept 3	**5,460**	**6,057**	**40,535**	**52,052**	**6,370**	**6,980**	**46,710**	**60,060**	**6,370**	**7,264**	**48,610**	**62,244**
Commuter Trips	5,460	-	-	5,460	6,370	-	-	6,370	6,370	-	-	6,370
Recreational Trips	-	6,057	40,535	46,592	-	6,980	46,710	53,690	-	7,264	48,610	55,874

Season is based on 26 weeks from May through October.
Commuter trips are based on a 5 day work week.
Commuters are charged $6 for a round trip fare based on regular use of service
Recreational users under 10yrs are charged $12 for a roundtrip fare.
Recreational users over 10 yrs are charged $20 for a roundtrip fare.

APPENDIX F

NPS D-303 / July 2005

www.ingramcontent.com/pod-product-compliance
Lightning Source LLC
Chambersburg PA
CBHW080413290526
45791CB00008BA/2256